THE PROMISE OF CULTURAL INSTITUTIONS

THE PROMISE
OF CULTURAL
INSTITUTIONS

DAVID CARR

ALTAMIRA
PRESS

A Division of Rowman & Littlefield Publishers, Inc.
Walnut Creek • Lanham • New York • Oxford

AltaMira Press
A Division of Rowman & Littlefield Publishers, Inc.
A wholly owned subsidary of the Rowman & Littlefield Publishing Group
1630 North Main Street, #367
Walnut Creek, CA 94596
www.altamirapress.com

Rowman & Littlefield Publishers, Inc.
A wholly owned subsidiary of the Rowman & Littlefield Publishing Group
4501 Forbes Boulevard, Suite 200
Lanham, MD 20706

PO Box 317
Oxford
OX2 9RU, UK

British Library Cataloguing in Publication Information Available

Library of Congress Cataloging-in-Publication Data

Carr, David, 1945–
    The promise of cultural institutions / David Carr.
      p. cm. — (American Association for State and Local History book
series)
    Includes bibliographical references and index.
    ISBN 0-7591-0291-0 (cloth : alk. paper) — ISBN 0-7591-0292-9 (pbk. : alk.
paper)
    1. United States—Cultural policy. 2. Libraries—Social aspects—United
States. 3. Museums—Social aspects—United States. 4. Learning and
scholarship—Social aspects—United States. 5. United States—Intellectual life.
6. Politics and culture—United States. 7. Art and state—United States.
I. Title. II. Series.
E169.12.C279 2003
306'.0973'074—dc21

                                                                                2002155808

Printed in the United States of America

♾™ The paper used in this publication meets the minimum requirements of
American National Standard for Information Sciences—Permanence of Paper
for Printed Library Materials, ANSI/NISO Z39.48-1992.

Contents

Acknowledgments, vii

Foreword, ix
by G. Rollie Adams

Introduction: Promises and Institutions, xiii

CHAPTER 1

A Museum Is an Open Work, 1

CHAPTER 2

Museums, Educative: An Encyclopedia Entry, 17

CHAPTER 3

In the Contexts of the Possible: Libraries and Museums
as Incendiary Cultural Institutions, 37

CHAPTER 4

A Community Mind, 55

CHAPTER 5

The Situation that Educates, 69

CHAPTER 6

A Poetics of Questions, 93

CHAPTER 7

Museums and Public Trust, 109

CHAPTER 8

Crafted Truths: Respecting Children in Museums, 131

CHAPTER 9

The Promise of Cultural Institutions, 155

CHAPTER 10

Ten Lessons and One Rule, 175

Appendix A: Selected Readings, 177

Appendix B: To Observe, 193

Appendix C: Each Life: Cultural Institutions
and Civic Engagement, 201

Index, 209

About the Author, 213

Acknowledgments

I gratefully acknowledge the following publishers and authors for their permission to reprint their publications: Taylor & Francis (www.tandf.co.uk) for "A Museum Is an Open Work," *International Journal of Heritage Studies* 7, no. 2 (2001): 173–183; the American Library Association for "In the Contexts of the Possible," *RBM: A Journal of Rare Books, Manuscripts and Cultural Heritage* 1, no. 2 (2000): 117–135, © 2000 by the American Library Association; the American Library Association for "A Community Mind," *Public Libraries* 41, no. 5 (2002): 284–288, © 2002 by the American Library Association; *Museum News*, the bimonthly magazine of the American Association of Museums for "Museums and Public Trust," *Museum News* (September/October 2001); Black Sparrow Press for Edward Field, "A Journey," in *Counting Myself Lucky: Selected Poems 1963–1992* (Santa Rosa, Calif.: Black Sparrow Press, 1992), © 1992 by Edward Field; the estate of Pablo Neruda and Copper Canyon Press for poems IX, XLIII, and XLIV from Pablo Neruda, *The Book of Questions* (Port Townsend, Wash.: Copper Canyon Press, 1991), © 1974 by Fundación Pablo Neruda, translation © 1991 by William O'Daly; New Directions Publishing Corporation for Eugene Guillevic, "Where," in *Selected Poems*, trans. Denise Levertov (New York: New Directions, 1969), © 1968, 1969 by Denise Levertov and Eugene Guillevic; Alfred A. Knopf, a division of Random House, Inc., for excerpts from W. S. Merwin, "Utterance," in *Rain in the Trees* (New York: Alfred A. Knopf, 1988);

and the authors of the student writing in chapter 9 for their work. Excerpts from "Style and Grace" and "The Work of Local Culture" from *What Are People For?* by Wendell Berry, © 1990 by Wendell Berry. Reprinted by permission of North Point Press, a division of Farrar, Straus and Giroux, LLC.

Foreword

David Carr would never use a cliché to make a point. He is much too eloquent a speaker and writer to resort to such a tactic. Nevertheless, the well-worn phrase "be all that you can be" comes quickly to mind as an accurate description of what he envisions for learners and the challenge he presents to those of us responsible for the promise of cultural institutions, particularly museums and libraries.

In our professional literature, "how to" books far outnumber "why to" books. This is a "why to" book. It reminds us why museums and libraries exist and what they have in common. It explores the power that redounds to both as places where knowledge and experience intersect. It calls upon us to expand our vision of the educational and life-enhancing potential that our institutions possess. And it articulates some key principles required to achieve that potential.

This book is about the need to enable learning. It is about meeting our users where they are and giving them the opportunity, encouragement, and tools necessary to make their own meanings within an informed context. It is about providing guests freedom to use our museums and libraries on their own terms, to select their own points of engagement with our learning environments, to access them through multiple learning styles, and to travel as fully or as quickly through them and their components as is individually desirable, stopping and starting as often as they want, passing over what does not appeal at any particular time, and delving and digging as deeply as they wish into whatever attracts. It is through these types of highly individual, creative, and very personal experiences that learning occurs. Each act of learning builds on preceding ones, and the learner is transformed, sometimes subtly and sometimes not so subtly, sometimes slowly and sometimes quickly, but always he or she grows.

This is also a "big picture" book. It is about recalling why we entered our professions and the obligation we have to support the learning of those we serve. This book reminds us that we support our users best by staying focused on the driving concepts of our work and not getting mired in its details. This book makes us understand that at the start of every day we need to remember that our primary task is not to complete the items on our daily agenda. Rather our primary task is to achieve the collective vision of our institutions, and their promise to enable learning.

Too often museums and libraries write strategic plans that are blueprints and then follow them either slavishly or not at all. An effective strategic plan is not a blueprint that identifies the place of every girder, screw, and nail, or every exhibit, program, and publication in a museum. Rather an effective strategic plan is a roadmap that points the way toward a destination and suggests the best routes to it, while at the same time allowing for optional pathways, and even the opportunity to circle back if necessary, in response to changing circumstances.

Blueprint mentality and day-to-day details obscure vision and promise. Roadmap planning and continued focus on driving concepts lead to the achievement of vision and promise. This book can help us keep on the better course. It can help us stay focused on our users.

This book is a work of both the mind and the heart. It is ideal for inspiration and a perfect foundation for strategic thinking and retreats. It prompts us to ponder whether we are giving our users all they want and need to become more effective learners, and it gives us inspiration, questions, counsel, and resources to help us ensure that we, indeed, are. It can help us realize the promise of our institutions.

G. Rollie Adams
President and CEO
Strong Museum
Rochester, New York

Here, where I am surrounded by an enormous landscape, which the winds move across as they come
from the seas, here I feel that there is no one anywhere
who can answer for you those questions and feelings
which, in their depths, have a life of their own; for
even the most articulate people are unable to help,
since what words point to is so very delicate, is almost
unsayable.

—Rilke, *Letters to a Young Poet*

Introduction: Promises and Institutions

A promise is an obligation to remember and carry out; it is a contract we make to meet the expectations of others, outside ourselves. A promise is not coerced; it is a free expression of will and engagement, a kind of gift. We may see in the idea of a promise something possible, but so far unrealized. A promise, by definition, exists in the future; it is not a fact or event. It is yet to be, a potential, a hypothesis, less a covenant than a hope. Until it has been kept and proven (the action taken, the knowledge given, the safety assured), the promise exists only in the contexts of the possible. That is the place I have in mind now as I write.

When I teach, I remind my students that cultural institutions are places created *to hold* and preserve objects and texts, *to expand* the boundaries of public knowledge associated with those artifacts and words, and *to open* the possibilities of learning in the contexts of everyday life. My teaching emphasizes learning in these places, and identifies them as parts of what educator and historian Lawrence Cremin calls the "configurations of education," meaning the multiplicity of institutions and individuals that educate."[1] In teaching, I try to evoke a generous world where we become ourselves through the gifts, experiences, and stories that reside in places and in people who are open and inviting to our presence, our eyes, and our questions.

I say to my students, as I say to my readers, that when we examine cultural institutions, we ought to consider their purposes, missions, and variations; their programs, espoused advocacies, and public dimensions; the forms of assistance and access offered by each; the ways we have of interacting with others in them; and how thoughtful use of cultural institutions can overcome the occasional barriers of elitism and distance that might discourage learners. I want my students to understand the countless and endless situations and practices that encourage reflection among users. We ought to think of the many paths a learner might follow in order to explore and master the forms of knowledge found in these places.

In all of our considerations, finally, I want my companions to think of the thoughtful user, the tasks of inquiry, and the personal transformations possible in the setting: the asking, thinking, and becoming that characterize the reflective life in process. We might consider the user to be a searcher, a creator of new paths and fresh connections, or simply a mind within a body surrounded by infinite sensations, contexts, and connections—sensations that encourage the learner toward self-renewal and reinvention.

When I define and apply the term *cultural institution*, I look for several things:

> *The presence of a collection*—a collection such as historical artifacts gathered from life; unique examples of rarities, like fine art or manuscripts; books and other forms of information; a preserved environment that captures a particular quality of life; living examples in some circumstances: plants, animals, fish; an unusual assemblage of artifacts that stimulate memories of a particular kind; or a monument or a memorial that communicates lessons to observers. These things—objects, living things, knowledge, information, contexts, lessons, memories—are all offered freely to people who seek them (whom we must always think of, with respect, as *users* or *learners*, not patrons or visitors) in the context of a systematic, continuous, organized knowledge structure.

A systematic, continuous, organized knowledge structure—a taxonomy, a series of relationships, a historical narrative, or the story of a life. Such a structure signifies that there is an inherent and invisible social and intellectual context for the collection, that it is apparent to the user with a little effort, and that it has appreciable depth and resonance, a richness to sustain attention, emphasizing in its structure, information, and substance the prevalent influence of scholarship, information, and thought.

Scholarship, information, and thought based on empirical experiences and observations, accurate information, documents and records, deep and significant content, and the suggestion of multiple contexts and implications. A certainty that *a culture of inquiry* and not commercialism, drives the environment, inviting people to enter, to linger, and to reflect on what they see and do there, without purchase of anything other, perhaps, than the way through the door.

I also ask my students to consider three themes, wherever we go and whatever we think about during the course of our work:

- public knowledge and memory

- adult independent inquiry and learning

- interdisciplinary connections and contexts of knowledge

These primary themes evoke a number of other ideas that I also ask my students to consider in the contexts of cultural institutions:

- permeable boundaries among disciplines

- pursuit skills needed by independent learners

- individual variants in cognitive styles

- the value of reflection and conversation in learning

- our desire for story, for a coherent narrative

- unknowns and unfinished issues to be invited as they appear to us

Most important, I emphasize that these themes and ideas—and the guiding questions connected to them—also occur as we lead our everyday lives outside the classroom, outside the museum, outside the library. Themes of inquiry, generosity, and integrity move through our learning lives as they do through our civic engagements and our characteristic individualities. I think that some of these are the unspoken themes that configure every life and give it depth—even though our conscious thoughts of them will be rare.

As an entire culture, however, we need to think steadily and seriously about adults and their learning needs in a world that can change with devastating gravity in less than a day. We need to consider and expand our promises to our own lives assuring that the best parts of them might grow and endure. We need to consider the possible first-person learning that might surround the reading of a novel or the daily newspaper, changes in our work, an unexpected physician's report, our regular encounters with technology, a sudden period of depression, the superb talk we can find on public radio, a new film, or the reading of a thoughtful analysis in a favorite magazine. Each evokes an authentic question, and in a small private voice we also hear an evocation of our integrity.

We need to regard others as learners and as potential teachers. When we meet people who display avocational or personal expertise in a practice or performance or art, we might want to ask, "Will you tell me how you learned this? What brings you to this challenge?" For brief moments, at least, we ought to allow knowledge to appear as our moving interest, if we are to understand the difference we might make by knowing more than we do.

Every person is, by definition, one part of a culture and so a constituent of the institutions it sustains. Consequently, we should each consider these places to mirror in some way the human experience as we can know it, or as we might wish to understand it. As adults, we are required to cultivate our own becoming, by investing ourselves in the possibilities of knowing something new and large on our own horizons. There is no substitute in one life for an interest in something outside it; in a learning world, we will always require a new problem of ourselves.

How do we understand an institution? How do we question our observations in order to make sense of them? How do people learn in museums and libraries? What can we learn in them? Why do we create and sustain such places? What drives the best of them? How do we evaluate them as settings for learning? What are their possible futures as providers of information and experience? What are the guiding missions we need in cultural institutions?

I see the museums and libraries of one life—the ones that have invited me and the ones I have invited myself to see—to have assisted me in living a better, less accidental, more reflective existence. It is a life that is more coherent, less isolated: a life with more purpose, and less fear, but a life always asking, and always essentially unfinished. It is a thinking life that often remembers great collections, and so it is a life that at times seems to be a collection itself.

Neither the treasures nor the information I have found in these places has made this difference. After my first steps among the objects and knowledge given in a museum or library, a specific setting and its collections become almost immaterial. Rapt and lost among things, I think of vanished hands and minds and am humbled by their traces: carved bone fragment, Breughel village, Cornell box, African burial effigy, *Moby Dick*. Each becomes a hand's work and a mind's work, and soon every place I see tells a history of hands and minds and their effects on the mutable world. Witnessing these human traces, and bearing them afterward in this way, has made a difference in me.

My life as a librarian and a teacher has given me a mission in the adoration and transfer of knowledge, a fascination with minds in play, and a devotion to the essential cognitive art, which is *connection*. Consequently, I am drawn to seek and praise the connective and the generous, or generative, acts of mind in every human place. These connections, too, may be thought of as hands shaping lives.

My dear colleagues in librarianship may find less about libraries in my work than they would wish, and more about museums than they care to read. My dear colleagues in museums may feel that I am apart from them in my work and preparation, and in my practice. From my earliest interests in museums, I have been guided by the genius of libraries and the gifted librarians I have known. My intention has been to address both institutions with one vocabulary, recognizing in them an identity of common motives and values. In my desire to suggest a pool of common values—collection, structure, education, inquiry, conviviality—I have, of course, thought often of the American community genius John Cotton Dana, the only heroic figure claimed by both cultural institutions.

I went to the library and to the museum for the same reason: I needed to grasp for myself the immaterial possibilities of the world and to make some of them my own, as a way to rescue myself from the everyday apprehension and insularity of being human. I went to these institutions because they are the magnificent secular treasures of the passionate learning life.

We all want an opportunity to feel smart and able, to feel that, even in the everyday, some bit of original wisdom is possible. We seek authenticity and integrity, solace and guidance, an idea of what other hands have constructed or other minds have made clear. Cultural institutions are the only places in our world where this can happen—not in television, film, radio, or school. Cultural institutions are the only places where a mindful experience can happen for everyone. And these experiences have happened as I have watched.

There is no choice for us as learners, if we are to live up to the possibilities of one life, other than to embrace our unfinished ideas and feelings and present them to ourselves, and perhaps to each other as evidences of our interior worlds. As learners, we must always make our worlds larger, particularly the worlds within, and we must become responsible for understanding the experiences they hold for us.

My opportunities as an educator and consultant have helped me develop grounded ideas about libraries and museums as situations for human transformation. Obligated by these opportunities and trusts, I have wanted to return the gifts and lessons. My students teach me to be hopeful and generous about all things. As one has said of learning together, "We take different things in and live different things out."

I have learned that excellence in cultural institutions means constant engagement in the problems of public knowledge. As proliferating themes of education and the culture of information remind us, what a culture knows, how it finds knowledge, and how it conducts its conversations about ethics, imagination, and policy are vital to its character and actions. These themes are also germane to understanding the promise of cultural institutions, where we can live out the unspoken parts of our experiences.

Consequently, over the past several years when I have met audiences—in Denver, Bozeman, Fort Worth, Wausau, Chicago, Winston-Salem, Indianapolis, Cleveland, Houston, New York, Washington, D.C., Philadelphia, Madison, Miami Beach, Charlottesville, Ithaca, Providence, Midland—I have done so as an advocate for the idea that we create and sustain these institutions because we want to become different people. We go to these places out of hope and will, and out of the desire for self-rescue.

Every learner must build a world that has never been built before and that will never be finished. Every learner must come to believe that experience permits us to possess something of our own that does not disappear.

The Promise of Cultural Institutions presents ten pieces, most prepared as spoken essays and read to professional audiences involved with many different cultural institutions. Writing out speeches is a way of assuring myself of a language that fits the task, and it prevents me from excessive improvising at the lectern. It is a comfort to have in hand what I want most to say, and it is a way to assure that the best words I have are given voice. Yet I remain fascinated by what cannot be given words, written or spoken. Museum and library experiences must all in some part hold a tacit experience (in Michael Polanyi's phrase, "the tacit dimension"[2]) at their center. As another epigraph in this collection implies, when we have come to understand deeply, words cannot tell our knowledge adequately to anyone.

It has taken me twenty years to grow accustomed to this monumental and abiding silence. This will always be a difficult truth for an essayist (or a professor) to accept. If we fill one void, however well, with talk and images, another opens, and it is likely to be even larger and more difficult to fill. The point is to look and think, at the edges of our senses, with whatever marginal language we may have, until we have crafted something not entirely silent for ourselves.

This collection is evidence that the gifts and experiences I have taken in over twenty years have required me at last to live out some of their lessons and processes in this form. This book has happened so slowly, and so much later in my life than I had once hoped. I am learning to be patient, as well as thankful, and to try to see the presumed patterns and meanings behind the *taking in* and the *living out*.

An invitation to join the faculty at the University of North Carolina at Chapel Hill, in the School of Information and Library Science, where I feel myself to be the most fortunate of teachers, has allowed me to find the strength to write and the courage to publish. I am indebted to my colleagues and my students, who have given me reasons to rescue myself as a scholar and writer.

I am particularly grateful for my colleagues and friends Jeffrey K. Smith, Jorge Schement, and Pat Leventhal. Every colleague in Chapel Hill has welcomed me, and given kindness and respect in addition to help. Dr. Robert Martin has invited me to speak twice under the aegis of the Institute for Museum and Library Services, in November 2001 (chapter 9) and October 2002 (appendix C), and I will always be grateful for his kindness in doing so.

Of all the places in which I have learned, the Strong Museum in Rochester, the Children's Museum in Indianapolis, the Metropolitan Museum of Art in New York, and the Brooklyn Museum of Art are paramount. Among my colleagues in museums, Paul Richard, Peter Sterling, Nikki Black, Carolyn Blackmon, Harold Skramstad, Rollie Adams, Scott Eberle, David Altshuler, David Henry, Elaine Gurian, Andrew Pekarik, and Zahava Doering have helped me understand the integrity of vision that must be present for constructed worlds to become vital worlds.

At the American Association of Museums, Ed Able has given me generous attention, and the editors of *Museum News*, John Strand and Jane Lusaka, have given me excellent advice and a place to be read. (The eighth chapter here is far better for Jane's case studies and revisions.) Twenty years ago, the late Malcolm Arth allowed me to wander freely in the Education Department at the American Museum of Natural History. Not long after, Dr. Arlon Elser of the W. K. Kellogg Foundation trusted me to visit many museums in that great foundation's name. Out of these generosities, my life has learned new things to say.

Although I have had no mentor in my life, there are people whose words and values have been with me for decades. The work and voice of Maxine Greene have offered inspiration without limit, and always will be close to my heart and mind. You will hear her voice in the essays here. Appendix A identifies many other writers who will always reside, with my gratitude, in any work of thought or advocacy I undertake.

Three people are at the center of my purpose for living: my family, Carol, Eve, and Anna; they have filled my heart every day with their grace, over time and distance. Many of my students reside in my heart, as well, some to stay forever, some yet to arrive—and so the heart grows. Because I think it would have pleased him to see it and hold it in his hands, this book is dedicated to my father, Clifford Wildon Carr. After almost forty years, I would love to hear his voice again.

Notes

1. Lawrence A. Cremin, *Public Education* (New York: Basic Books, 1976), 30.

2. Michael Polanyi, *The Tacit Dimension* (New York: Anchor Books, 1967).

1

A Museum Is an Open Work

I see the museum as I see the library: a mind-producing system, perhaps an organism, an embodiment of a larger, shaping cultural mind, but also an embodiment of intentional connections and cultural possibilities. Large as it may be, the museum can be an intimate frame for our lives, what we think of them, and what we want them to become. Perhaps even more so than the library, the museum is an institution devoted to emerging thoughts, including some that do not appear for days or weeks or long after using the museum. Certainly the museum holds things in place for us, so our minds might move toward, surround, look back at, consider, and reconsider them. The work of the museum is the revelation of artifacts and texts. It is also the revelation and embodiment of tacit subtexts and more private, whispered, unspoken, perhaps unspeakable, meanings or feelings.

The museum is a place for the *construction* of meanings and their integration into the knowledge and experience one has; beyond this, the museum *itself* is a construction of meanings. Nothing is there by accident, not even its users. *At its best*, a museum offers a constructed situation, a place we seek out purposefully, in order to explore and revise the formative messages we intend to gather about ourselves, engaged as we always are in the process of self-identification, our *own* process of construction.

None of these motives is likely to be spoken aloud. In this constructed situation, we silently seek objects that engage our attention, demand our reflection, and lead us to interpretations, even if we may keep their power over us secret from ourselves. Our experiences change and reconstruct us. More than schools, museums help transform us into what we are meant to become, because we willingly dwell in them out of a deeper, more integrated need in our lives. Museums also provide situations where we can select experiences for our own learning selves and define the most engaging frames for our cognitive acts, from recognition to puzzlement to diving deep. Capturing and holding far more than the sum of their visible contents, museums enfold the multiple, infinite, and simultaneous constructions of their users. It is in museums, far better than in other cultural institutions, that people may assume the greatest responsibility for both the *process* and *authorship* of the meanings they produce.[1]

Elliot Eisner writes about his own journey as a scholar and an artist:

> I came to believe that perception is a cognitive event and that construal, not discovery, is critical. Put another way, I came to believe that humans do not simply have experience; they have a hand in its creation, and the quality of their creation depends upon the ways they employ their minds. A second idea that has guided my journey is the belief that the use of mind is the most potent means of development. What we think about matters. What we try to do with what we think about matters.[2]

It is from Eisner's citation of Basil Bernstein that the first words of this essay, about the museum as a mind-producing organism, have been borrowed.

In a museum, "what we try to do with what we think about" is to engage in sequences of relationships with objects, texts, and other human beings, followed by pauses, reflections, evaluations, and plans. We might consider the museum to be an open system in part because of what the user brings to these encounters: a history as a learner, an evolving repertoire of private memory, a malleable scheme of the world, a self-designed desire to become different.

The user also brings a capacity for awe but also an articulate language to *undo* that awe and explain its power. The great experience at times begs to be understood and spoken aloud to others. These alternations of activity, reactivity, and expression are parts of the human need and presence that complete the museum and cause it to become part of the user's lived experience.

Completing the museum through thought and speech is, for its users, a way to advance cognitive activities, to connect encountered information to a personal design, and to tie what is newly seen to the lasting stories in our minds. It is a way to try out new information in a relatively safe environment, where intellectual and experiential risk can be sustained and nurtured. It is also a way to engage in cognitive play and adaptation, a way of leaning forward into the emerging idea, the "not-yet" (a term I borrow from Maxine Greene), or the not-yet-fully-understood.

These observations always occur to me when I stand within the structure of any museum, embedded as its participant. There, I engage in reflective observations. I present myself to the entire structure and select from its parts. I respond to, and so I create, this environment, not as an operator or a visitor, but as an actor and thinking receiver. I *use* the museum to transform myself. Even while I am *in* the museum, I think that my task is to reconstruct the setting and the concepts in my own vision and frame, and to savor in detail the small tensions and transfers of meaning, the cognitive news, the forces of thought and imagination that allow me to travel here and beyond.

The institution and I are interdependent, and mutually inspired: it is a dynamic knowledge structure, and I am a dynamic cognitive structure. I bring my energies to every moment, expecting to be met by a challenge, an unknown, some exquisite thing. I make cognitive moves among what I know and do not know. Knowing this, remembering that, expecting something, being astonished and fascinated, being bored, falling backward, forcing myself ahead: this is what I do here.

As an actor and thinking receiver in the museum, my work is to test and direct the flow of my own ideas, and at times it is my task to move against that flow, to avoid the familiar, to overcome the constraints of the situation and my own inadequate responses to it. I move with my own best questions, my pauses and reflections, my tentative perceptions of meaning. My task is, in the midst of this, to reconstruct and reassemble the situation I have been given, controlling and recombining its elements as I need them most to be. With luck, I am surprised. With great luck, I am astonished.

But to be astonished, I often must strive to go far beyond what the museum gives me. In some places I need to restore a context the museum has removed, and I must often find for myself a language the museum has withheld. And so you have my topic, and its multiple facets: the user *completing* the museum as a cognitive environment, the user *informing* the museum as a figure within its system of meanings, the user *going beyond* the museum into the surrounding environment, and the user *becoming the mindful author* of one life, engaged by the museum in an experience of the new.

I am most interested in the museum user turning away from accidental life, and toward intentional experiences that move thought forward—experiences that transmit possibility and move the person closer to crafting the meanings of things. I am interested in the natural and stimulated course of thoughts in cultural institutions, and in the satisfaction of continuing interests. I am interested in human minds as they take form, minute by minute, and in the experiences they wish to understand more completely, and carry away in memory.

I consider all cultural institutions as structures alike in the deep and infinite array of possibilities they hold for the reflective design of one life. But I recognize, as well, the immanent possibilities every museum contains for the exquisite surprise, the challenge to assumptions, even for anguish and pain. I most respect the power of the museum that causes us not only to see intensely, but also to leave informed and transformed. In some ways, I feel that museum use should be most like the experience of reading a vivid novel, say one by Gabriel García Márquez, in that we perform the experiences we have as clearly and intensely as we can, as though they were dances, in the worlds within our heads.[3]

The tension between our designs and our astonishments is the kind of play that allows us to think of museums as transformative learning systems, places where our fresh reflections, insights, and second thoughts allow us to become aware of our own progress and the sudden critical keys to our emergence as learners. Jack Mezirow refers to these as "emancipatory" experiences.[4]

The museum offers its users a system of potentially emancipatory experiences: opportunities to be present among inspired objects and to find in the traces of inspiration a transforming sense of human action and construction. When the museum gathers and gives at its best, it may also offer us a confrontation with authenticity we might wish at that moment to turn away from. Nearly every object, and certainly every exhibition, ought to assist us to use what we witness as we ask our own critically probing questions about it.

In how many ways might this have meaning to you? In this opening-up, the museum makes a deeply challenging experience possible. This is the experience that matters most to museum use. The purpose of the museum at its best is, like the purpose of a great educator, to cause some kind of troubling incompleteness for the user, and so to inspire human pursuit and gradual change.

Encounters begin obviously. At the early edges of our museum experiences, we are given objects and texts, things to see and perhaps touch, objects in relation to other objects. But we are also given objects in relation to our memories and longings, and language we can use to evoke what we see and understand. While we may encounter a complex public documentation in museum objects and their surroundings—patterns, details, makers, and meanings—we also encounter simultaneous and more complex, *private* dimensions of our own memories, resonances, and mysteries.

Such privacies can be invited and encouraged. For every word of public curatorial language in the museum, there are countless, ephemeral private utterances and wordless thoughts that regulate our attentions and feelings, often having nothing to do with the curator's language. This is what ought to happen; part of the museum's responsibility is to create situations for our private language *not* to disappear, but to be given an articulated voice. An immediate and personal language is important for both the museum and the museum user, because every object (whatever history surrounds it) exists first for us in the present. With each new encounter with an object (no matter how rich the information given to us), the initial mystery is always fresh. Further, as Lev Vygotsky suggests, the private speech we use is a primary perceptual act.[5] It will later become our denotative language and the structural center of our personal cognitive record. It is too important to be lost or replaced by even the most accurate curatorial words.

We must be cautious about the conventional language of museums, found so often in panels and labels and catalogs. "There is no guarantee that the way language seems to divide up the world reflects the way the world is constructed. Language," says writing theorist Frank Smith, "merely reflects our way of trying to make sense of the world."[6] In a chapter titled "The Thought Behind Language," Smith writes useful words about the idea of mystery:

> I do not know why we are so reluctant to acknowledge mystery, especially since the world seems so full of it in so many fundamental ways. Children are rarely taught about mystery, although I am sure they understand and respect it. Instead we tend to encourage them to believe that only knowledge exists.[7]

Where is the museum that emphasizes what we do not yet know? Where might we hear a voice suggest intriguing unknowns or unresolved questions surrounding its objects? That might be the most educative, transformative museum of all, and it is possible everywhere we look.

The best museum encounters may begin obviously, but perhaps they must then proceed uneasily. At the edge of the museum we are given opportunities to attend with care, to inquire as best we can. We are given small chances to experience and speculate as ways to possess the object and become a tentative participant—a critical observer, perhaps—in its existence. But generally, our experiences are limited by the museum. In the presence of museum objects, we are kept at a distance and given opportunities for only mental, imagined touch. Greater intimacy with the object is of course reserved for the curator who is too often silent about the knowledge most pertinent to the object—how it feels, how it compares to others, how it ignites the senses.[8] And so we must improvise.

Always at a distance, it is only by the intensity of our thought and gaze, and by the fertility of our memories, that we can carry our meanings about and make of them something resembling coherence, continuity, or pattern. Using the familiar metaphor of woven fabric, an applicable idea of coherence in an educational museum frame has been described by Margret Buchmann and Robert Floden.

> Educational coherence depends on patterns and loose ends; on materials, animating ideas, and formative activities. Threads interlace, but there are fuzzy bits and dangling strands of experience and meaning, with outworn or thin patches being worked over or unraveled over time. Resulting from the way it is woven, a fabric may be strong and matted or filmy and insubstantial. . . . Educational coherence is found where students can discover and establish relations among various areas of sensibility, knowledge, and skill, yet where loose ends remain, inviting a reweaving of beliefs and ties to the unknown.[9]

In museums we are engaged in the weaving of our own fabrics, combining new and increasingly complex strands, even while we are wearing them. We are weaving, and also designing, tailoring, and adjusting them to fit, while we are within.

A museum's system can also be understood as a fabric. Its themes and language, its recognizable values and its stance toward its users, even its open ends and unexplored assumptions, communicate the rhythmic textures of a system. These qualities will differ from place to place. We often stand in the midst of such museum systems, yet we are unable to understand the patterns that control them and the themes that move through them and carry us along. We often cannot see where they might lead us next.

Speaking as a librarian who now struggles to grasp the value and function of an edgeless and challenging electronic information world, I recall a time when it was possible to understand information from the outside and to design cognitive experiences with a sense of control and purpose. Now, among complex, everyday information technologies and the ambiguous nature of inquiry, we must strive to understand and experiment from within those often bland and featureless landscapes. These experiences are increasingly difficult to frame.

Standing inside the museum, immersed in a structure of objects and knowledge, we are challenged to find our own way, to move logically forward in the most constructive directions, to gather usable language and rules of discourse, to look and think and talk critically, and (echoing Donald Schön) to collaborate as in a conversation with the informing situation we occupy.[10] Reflection of this kind occurs within a generally unexamined part of museum use, the pause. Frank Smith, again writing about the writer, points out that our understandings of "events are the products of contemplation, not action. When we are involved in action, in interaction, then we have no awareness."[11] Only by withdrawing can we find the language of our experience and respond to the information we have encountered. Through simple means, museums can construct these pauses with a consistency of purpose. The pause is important because nothing happens in it.

As an inquirer in the museum, my own process is to gather evidence using a series of ethnographic questions, starting with "What's going on here? What information is present here? How *is* information defined and given here?" These evidently simple questions are actually quite complex, and the knowledge they yield is often unclear. I need the pause to address the problems I have given myself. In the museum, as in every situation where it matters, information is neither neutral nor merely expansive. It carries an agenda; it has both didactic and aesthetic dimensions; it may be political; it must be understandable as both logic and art. Information in the museum is not benign: its purpose is to inspire friction, start fires, build problems, and invite critical inquiry. Unless this happens, nothing human happens and no one learns.

It is possible to see museum use as an experience in problem solving. We begin to construct the problem of the museum in the first few minutes of our presence. What has been brought here? What might I see or experience? What do such objects mean? What here is unknown to me? What information is given to me? What are its origins? Did a human being make it? Of what system or structure is it a part? What does it contribute to the living of one life? What values surround it? What story can be told to explain it? How does it change me? With its absence, what would be missing in the world?[12]

My naive questions echo many other formal and informal museum heuristics, all intended to suggest that in every object we might find the art of the distant maker, the ideas of design and function, and the surroundings of memory and experience. They are my ways of seeking the *resonant implications* within the unfamiliar. Here Stephen Greenblatt describes the idea of resonance in his memory of the "precarious" even "vulnerable" objects in the Jewish Museum in Prague.

> A resonant exhibition often pulls the viewer away from the celebration of isolated objects and toward a series of implied, only half-visible relationships and questions. . . . This museum is not so much about artifacts as about memory, and the form memory takes is a secularized Kaddish, a commemorative

prayer for the dead. . . . This resonance depends not upon visual stimulation but upon a felt intensity of names, and behind the names, as the very term resonance suggests, of voices: the voices of those who chanted, studied, muttered their prayers, wept, and then were forever silenced.[13]

Greenblatt's awareness of resonance makes clear that even the most delicate negotiations of meaning in one's life have more than momentary power. The concept recognizes that every person harbors unresolved issues and unexplored territories, and that, in cultural institutions, every person needs access to the story that will best assist these sensory explorations. The museum offers its users an invitation to guide, connect, and construct their own cognitive or emotional developments, and to risk the possibilities of becoming whomever they would become, beyond themselves as they are, different from who they were. The invitation is for the museum exhibition to become an event in the mental life of the user. I observe that, given an inviting, resonant opportunity, people will accept, will open an experience for themselves, pause as they need, and close it at the point of saturation.

Sometimes the museum and its objects may constitute an experiential event, engaging the user as a system for the senses. Or the museum may become an informing agency, where the data given can surround and pervade the user's experience, like an absorbing text. Or the museum may become a challenge to critical thinking, offering fresh perspectives on a great problem, or suggesting alternative ways to think about everyday things. Or, the museum may offer a cognitive event of great complexity by presenting an exquisite, resonant question we can never fully answer—even though the user's full experience is brought to bear, contextualizing, comparing, adducing, juxtaposing, evaluating, and recognizing relevant evidence far beyond the museum. The greatest possibility of such brief but complex events is that they will become unforgettable.

Challenging cognitive situations where people are encouraged to strive toward meaning are countless in cultural institutions. They foster a tendency to think twice, to seek more information, and perhaps to plan an independent inquiry. But it is also clear that these countless stimulating situations often fail to support and sustain the intellect when the simplest devices—bibliographies, pamphlets, quotations, critical controversies, news items, the unanswered questions of the day—would carry the user into a future of new perspectives and possibilities.

Under museum circumstances, where the situation is designed to be always incomplete and where new information continuously flows in, the museum begins to live up to the best of its users, those who are seized—enraptured—by objects and their implications, and who stand (or hover) momentarily on the edge of insight. These are museum users at the point of transformation toward active, guiding engagement in the design of something new for themselves. And in that willingness to seize and be seized by ideas, the best of its users live up to the open possibilities of museums.

In an essay titled "The Poetics of the Open Work," Umberto Eco discusses modern instrumental music compositions requiring autonomous interpretation by the performer, who decides how long to hold a note, its tonality, and the form of the whole piece. Eco cites one composer who describes his composition as "not so much a musical composition as a *field of possibilities*, an explicit invitation to exercise choice."[14]

In this same sense, the museum is an open work, created only in the play of its users, who are free to perform and communicate individual or collaborative experiences of objects and situations according to their own designs. What do I want most to know here, today? What has been most interesting in the past? Where can I pause to reflect? What do I want to remember about what I experience, in order to communicate about it later? What connection does this make to the outer world? Every user completes the museum as an open work in a different way and pursues its ideas and information in a wholly personal configuration.

Even in modest museum environments, these possible individual performances must constantly expand the meanings of the museum, and they are unlikely to exhaust it easily. If we imagine larger, more complex museums as open works, the possible performances of meaning they suggest may be infinite. However, the structures of the museum as an open work should help the user to frame a horizon or an array of the possibilities it holds.

When we stand at the edge of something unknown, we need the value of an insightful idea, or a human model of active thinking, or a contrasting example, or a provocative comment by a nearby voice. Any of these stimuli can inspire a new point of view. Stimulated by such connections, suggestions, quotations, or concepts, it is likely that users will seek more information. Through an architecture of questions, risks and possibilities, thinking users will arrive over time at their own sustained, crafted truths.

Great institutions and their learners are mutually permeable. Inevitably, the museum where crafted truths can occur is grounded on profound respect and responsibility for the cognitive experiences of its users. In cultural institutions of all kinds, it is always useful to envision the user who would want to know of objects and resources available, other than those on display; who would want to be able to consult at times with an experienced other person; who would want to know what to read; who might want to be connected to others thinking in similar ways; who might need help in learning how to resolve difficult questions; who might need access to the curator's thoughts; who might want to write, photograph, draw; or who might need to experience and understand related contexts. It is possible as well that, beyond these basic suggestions and supports, the museum might invite its users to participate directly in the construction of the museum's leading ideas, the themes that define and enrich its fabric.

The work of the museum—like Vygotsky's concept of the "more advanced peer,"[15] beckoning and assuring the less-experienced learner—is to broaden the possibilities of a person's response, to create ways for users to examine their own insightful experiences in museums (so they might have more of them), to assist unspoken questions to emerge in forumlike conversations, and to provide other services for the exploration and use of uncertainties expressed directly in the users' own questions.

_____ ⸏as been a visionary, articulate advocate for ⸍of youth in the openness of the museum. His description of the relationship between institution and user applies across museums and libraries, and across generations.

> Young people need a place that they sense is their own. They need to have a part in the design and organization of that space. They need to help establish the procedures and operate the space in accordance with their ideas about success. . . . At every level the program will be "with" young people instead of simply "for" them. . . . One of the key ingredients for adolescent programs is to create experiences that are legitimate opportunities for valid participation. Exhibitions can be conceived, designed, and installed by young people. . . . Museums can provide a working environment where youngsters who are not traditionally asked to be partners can analyze power structures, authority, decision making, group dynamics. . . . Building mutual trust and respect is just the beginning. In order to empower these adolescents, museums must address what is often their most critical need: valuing themselves.[16]

The idea of valuing the individual self, savoring the private experience, the ability to construct knowledge and possibility for oneself—all ways to hear the resonances of one life—seems to stand as a universal need.

To see the museum as an open work is to recognize that it is always discovered by its users in an unfinished state, not unlike seeing it as a laboratory, or a workshop for cognitive change. It is a setting where the museum may offer tools, materials, and processes for systematic, exploratory approaches to experience and purposeful thought. These are acts that might lead one further, toward insight, and toward the occasional, exquisite, transforming surprise. Further, the great museum allows its users an opportunity to understand, through reading or conversation, the insights and transformations of others. The great museum assists its users to ask—and to answer—the question, What transformations are possible for good learners here?

In the very act of presenting itself, every museum becomes committed to a narrative about the construction of its world, with several parts: the transformation of vision into artifact or prototype; new reconstruction of the biological or anthropological record; the history of habitation in a specific site; the processes that regulate everyday lifework; the strides of technology; the evocation and transmission of memory. Every museum user needs the opportunity to move, mind and body, into the narrative until it merges with the user's own.

If, as Clifford Geertz writes, "The culture of a people is an ensemble of texts,"[17] the museum can be seen as the convergence of a culture's confluent strands—commerce, history, education, art, craft, heroism, innovation, personality, genius, failure. In its objects are the stories of their makers, working in the everyday world, striving to imagine and interpret its possibilities through their art. Is it not possible that, in this way, all of our stories are held in the museum's objects, whether they are the narratives of our passions, our reveries, or our play?

To bring an example to the conclusion of this essay, I offer Joseph Kosuth's early nineties installation at the Brooklyn Museum, *The Play of the Unmentionable*, an assemblage of works, texts, and subtexts surrounding the body, eroticism, and censorship. The exhibition and the published volume that documents it offer memorable evidence that sharp-edged exhibitions are equally conceptual and physical events, where texts illuminate the integrity of objects with fitting and provocative ideas.[18] The exhibition brought the responsive human into the play (that is to say, into the work) of the museum, by using texts and juxtapositions to illuminate the possible meanings of artworks as cultural summaries. Inevitably, by design, Kosuth allowed some of that light to flow over the edges onto the assumptions and values of the witness, the user. The exhibition itself drew many thousands to the Brooklyn Museum, suggesting the public's awakened appetite for complexity, engagement, and mindful questioning.

Reviewing the published version of this exhibition, I wrote

> As witnesses, when we find that we have thought the unthinkable, we have become complicit in the work of art, and so we

must redefine ourselves and our possible worlds. Certain things we hold within our hearts and minds—from tacit assumptions to active lusts—are unmentionable because to say them would cause us to forego our carefully crafted identities and redefine ourselves as human beings. Here, in Kosuth's work, this redefinition of ourselves is essential to the museum's effect, because we complete the exhibition in our minds, and deal there with the lasting trouble it causes us. [The experience demonstrated] the completeness of self-understanding that art provokes and we cannot deny.[19]

Our best learning becomes most possible in the museum when humans are moved to the edges of their experiences, to the point where everything that lies before them is unknown, where they must pay new forms of attention, where a momentary insight can reorganize parts of knowledge completely, and where the interpretation of the narrative involves the beginnings of a new conversation about how one life might move forward after this experience. In this open work of a museum, whenever we encounter and enter its possibilities and then open ourselves in response, we are assisted to find powers of thought and speech with an integrity that we may have previously concealed, even from ourselves.

Notes

An early version of this work was first presented at the Cybernetics in the Art of Learning Conference, American Society for Cybernetics, Philadelphia, November 5, 1993. Another version appeared in the *International Journal of Heritage Studies* 7, no. 2 (2001): 173–183.

1. See Joseph Kosuth, *Art after Philosophy and After* (Cambridge, Mass.: MIT Press, 1991), 220.

2. Eliot Eisner, "Forms of Understanding and the Future of Educational Research," *Educational Researcher* 22, no. 7 (1993): 5.

3. The last phrase in this sentence is Frank Smith's. See Frank Smith, *Writing and the Writer* (New York: Holt, Rinehart & Winston, 1981).

4. See Jack Mezirow and Associates, *Fostering Critical Reflection in Adulthood* (San Francisco: Jossey-Bass, 1990); Jack Mezirow, *Transformative Dimensions of Adult Learning* (San Francisco: Jossey-Bass, 1991).

5. Lev S. Vygotsky, in *Mind in Society: The Development of Higher Psychological Processes*, ed. Michael Cole, et al. (Cambridge, Mass.: Harvard University Press, 1978), 32–33.

6. Smith, *Writing and the Writer*, 29.

7. Smith, *Writing and the Writer*, 27.

8. See Mihaly Csikszentmihalyi and Rick E. Robinson, in *The Art of Seeing: An Interpretation of the Aesthetic Encounter* (Malibu, Calif.: J. P. Getty Museum, 1990), 27–71.

9. Margret Buchmann and Robert Floden, "Coherence, the Rebel Angel," *Educational Researcher* 21, no. 9 (1992): 8.

10. Donald A. Schön, *The Reflective Practitioner* (New York: Basic Books, 1983), 76.

11. Smith, *Writing and the Writer*, 43.

12. See David Carr, "Minds in Museums: The Cognitive Management of Cultural Institutions," *Teachers' College Record* 93, no. 1 (Fall 1991): 6–27.

13. Stephen Greenblatt, "Resonance and Wonder," in *Exhibiting Cultures: The Poetics and Politics of Museum Display*, ed. Ivan Karp and Steven D. Lavine (Washington, D.C.: Smithsonian Institution Press, 1991), 45–47.

14. Umberto Eco, *The Open Work* (Cambridge, Mass.: Harvard University Press, 1989), 1.

15. Lev S. Vygotsky, *Mind in Society*, 84–85.

16. Peter Sterling, "Young and Promising," *Museum News* 72, no. 6 (1993): 43.

17. Clifford Geertz, *The Interpretation of Cultures* (New York: Basic Books, 1973), 452.

18. Joseph Kosuth, *The Play of the Unmentionable* (New York: The New Press, 1992).

19. David Carr, review of *The Play of the Unmentionable*, by Joseph Kosuth, *Museum News* 72, no. 4 (July/August 1993): 21–23, 62.

2

Museums, Educative:
An Encyclopedia Entry[1]

A Definition

An educative museum is a cognitive environment, a collection of objects and ideas configured by and for exploratory human minds, where intellectual change happens as experiences are constructed by the questions of its users.

These questions are likely to be unspoken; they may be invisible, hidden in the way a museum user selects experiences and observes objects. They may be founded on an evanescent, momentary unknown. A new door opens, or an open door reveals surprises, and the mind is invited to attend to something previously unseen.

Or questions may follow an experience, drawn from a deep and continuing inquiry, a permanent search carried on over a lifetime. Or the user's questions may have the patterns of a kaleidoscope or a constellation, taking new forms around a set of multiple, connected, recurrent unknowns. These are the questions we ask over and over, the unfinished issues of an individual life.

An educative museum encourages and assists the individual user, the one who strives toward a consequential presence, who sustains attention to things and the concepts that surround them. An educative museum—or any educative cultural institution—creates a functional structure for cognitive change.

Here, *educative* means *tending to educate*, or tending to support the person inclined toward inquiry, and it is in this sense that learners do not *visit* museums—they *use* them. Any cultural institution is educative when it creates situations that invite, support, and expand independent inquiry without imposing the procedures, curricula, evaluations, or instructions of classrooms or the remote electronic impersonality of distance learning. An institution is educative when it offers the user an array of possibilities to experience, then offers a path to useful examples and interpretations of the evidence, and then encourages the user toward sustained reflection and new planning.

An educative museum nurtures and engages the museum user with authoritative information, alternative interpretations, and direct experiences. Expanding the meanings of objects and cultures, an educative museum addresses the future thoughts and insights of its users, offering them contexts, resources, and processes that induce new perspectives, even among familiar things.

An educative museum develops, maintains, and opens its collections in the name of the public, for the use of the public, and for public understanding. Against time and damage, it preserves things and assures them an enduring presence in a world not yet born. The museum surrounds its objects with relevant information, aimed to lead the user toward insights about knowledge, artistry, and endeavor. The museum and its contents are constructed as a systematic setting for the connection of human beings to rare objects of value and power. Through proximity to artifacts and experiences, an educative museum creates circumstances for informing, illuminating, and exploring knowledge.

The User in the Educative Museum

In the midst of a complex life, perhaps with few resources other than memories and questions, the user enters a museum, alone or with companions, carrying expectations of something extraordinary about to happen. Perhaps the user hopes to discover or create a difference in familiar experiences and thoughts. Perhaps the user has one exhibition, or one object, in mind. Perhaps the user has an hour to kill. Whatever draws this user to the museum, and whatever questions, contexts, and memories enter simultaneously, the museum receives this person and this situation.

The user stands on the edge of the museum, tentative, unsure of the best beginning, moving forward question by silent question. The user is inspired or awed by an idea, or simply curious, ready to transform observations, information, or astonishment into constructed meanings.

When original thinking and learning happen for the user, in the presence of a resourceful system of objects and data, the situation is likely to include a mix of questions, memories, and constraints. As the person moves on a path through the physical museum space, a path through the mind is walked as well. Every step among the museum's objects and texts has the potential to evoke a relationship between the user and information, between the moment and a memory. It may be an unexplored idea embedded in past thoughts, or it may be a formative curiosity or emptiness left behind by schooling.

The most productive relationship to information may be the simple wondering that begins, What is there to know about this? Such wondering guides and inflects individual experiences across the lifespan. In a museum, amid the potential for many encounters with great works or challenging insights, these traces may be at their most resonant and influential.

Entering the museum, the adult learner almost immediately asks and decides about steps to be taken, becomes an explorer of inviting and echoing ideas, and thinks like a designer of something new among experiences. This is rarely a simple engagement; the educative museum is various, largely unmapped, and nonroutine. Each emergent museum experience holds and evokes complex possibilities and risks of change.

To think in the presence of new experience, to learn from the unexpected encounter, or to grasp a whole civilization through its remnant artifacts is to stand at a thinking edge made imminent by proximity and authenticity. The educative museum causes learners to be present among challenging objects and ideas, and more important, to become immediate witnesses to their own cognitive transformations.

At this edge, museum users have many needs. There is the need to find a point of orientation, in order to begin. There is the need to seek information about the array and its organization. There is the need to survey options for moving through the museum. There is the need to anticipate constraints of time and space. There is the need to consider a pattern or a plan, a strategy for engagement, to try out and follow or alter until the experience takes on the logics and meanings of a whole encounter.

For the museum user, every path taken is a tacit course of inquiry, an asking and seeking for something that lies ahead, an anticipation of something about to happen or a remembering of something that has. The best museum experiences may have the sudden, unplanned qualities of hunting, or the experimentation and daring of artistry, or the pleasures of a savory meal. The museum may lead to exotic, unexpected connections; it may lead to grieving and distress; it may lead to new insights and possibilities. But first, it is likely to be an experience of thought and design.

Museums and Knowledge

Under educative leadership, collections in museums can become profound cognitive instruments, committed to display the works and issues of a culture, and to make them available in ways that inspire connected thoughts.

Museum collections permit the observer to see rare examples of wholeness: the exemplary works of an individual artist; objects assembled from their own time, place, and civilization; the varieties of a species; the possessions of multiple generations and multiple families; or the meanings of a single event in its time and contexts.

Museums can capture whole perspectives, offer variations on themes, and assist diverse reflections from unusual points of view. Within the museum's gatherings and explanations, patterns can be made apparent and structures or processes can be demonstrated. For nearly every apparent truth the museum offers, there is an illustrative variation or a confirming exemplar to be placed before us as well.

It is possible for a museum collection to surround an idea or concept, an era, a period of social or technical transition, and to expose its consequences in an array of physical forms. Using samples taken across centuries and presented in a narrative, or given to users in restored contexts, an innovation, an abstraction, or an invisible process can become observable. The presentation of cultural objects or empirical observations can expose or clarify the meaning of critical skills and techniques. Ecologies, economies, families, and social structures surround every great change, and conditions of life are renewed or thwarted in its wake. Museums can document the differences among specific landscapes, geographies, nations, and societies. They can display contrasts not only in materials, tools, and objects, but also in stances toward the human condition, the construction of knowledge, and the meanings of individual lives embedded in places we may never otherwise see.

Collections, grounded in ideas, open to observation, and supported by sound information, can create differences in the user. When museums provide rich contextual information among objects, the experience extends ideas we may have first encountered in less immediate and more impersonal places such as the media, the web, or a classroom. Collections that display challenging cultural contexts can open an observer's eyes to the connections among objects and environments and the direct lines between lives and societies.

When provocative museum collections inspire discourse and other personal transactions among companions, useful things happen. The revelation of differing, multifaceted perspectives becomes possible. Perceptions and details can be directly apprehended, discussed, and disputed. Among contextual clues, pervasive ambiguities, unanswered questions, and multiple interpretations, an independent learner's sense of intellectual autonomy—the power to see information and decide about the truth, to explore the evidence directly—is greatly expanded.

We often struggle to see clearly. Our questions come from situations where unambiguous meanings are often difficult to extract and unify. Our memories and constraints tell us that a clear image of our own knowledge is elusive and always subject to negotiation with what is at hand. To live a life of caring inquiry is the primary way to integrate these reflective negotiations with experience, and to give them focus. In an educative museum, good questions—and the responsive acts that surround them—can lead the thoughtful learner toward intellectual integrity.

Educative museum experiences are grounded in the objects and structures, and in the collections and values, of an institution. More important than these, learning and thinking in the museum are grounded in the active constructions of an asking mind. Entering the museum, this mind is formative and incomplete; it bears memories and expectations, a history of educational successes and disasters, a fluid repertoire of seamless knowledge and information, patterns of attending to new data, an educative style, and a cluster of unfinished inquiries that draw the user toward something that remains to be seen.

The Museum as an Intellectual Problem

The fresh mind emerging in the museum is expansive, connective, convergent, open to adjustments and variations. It is also rare; a conventional life often tends to create narrow boundaries for learning. There are often too many burdens to leave behind at the museum door. People come to museums within hard economies of time, attention, and communication; this is sometimes softened by encouraging companionship, active interests, and manageable distances. The arrival of a fresh mind is not to be assumed. We should assume, instead, that every learning mind needs to find its way through a wilderness of constraints, possibilities, and alternatives.

An educative museum requires an inspired learner, a person whose thoughts are in motion. Part of the gift of the museum to its users must be a trust established before their arrival: the museum's promise to regard the human being as a learner who will be respected and assisted and who will be given the best of the museum's offerings. By opening itself to the user as an agency for learning, the museum becomes an invitational world, the only kind of place where learning can happen. Once opened, a museum can be seen as a series of inviting problems of attention, focused thoughts, and insightful connections among complex objects and information. It communicates: Reflection is possible here.

As a problem-solving experience, intentional museum use requires the user to understand both the present opportunities for learning and the tacit possibilities for their exploration.

> *What is at hand?* Objects and texts. These may be easily accessible, or they may be difficult to see and more difficult to understand. They may be complex and challenging to define.
>
> *What information is given?* Some objects may be presented without contexts. Some explanations may be obscure and private, for scholars only; they may answer questions the museum user has not asked, or is unlikely to ask.
>
> *What deserves our best attention?* Museum objects are likely to be unequal in aesthetic, empirical, or historic importance, so the user must learn to attend to them in different ways.
>
> *Where does a learner begin?* Certain pieces or ideas may be primary and essential; a good strategy starts with them, if they can be identified.
>
> *What does a learner need to know?*
>
> *What is a museum user to think about these things?*

In responsive museums, these questions have been anticipated, and the idea of *the learner learning* has been given public attention. What do learners need? Resources for asking and pursuing their own inquiries. Help that confirms intellectual integrity. Confidence in the motive that impels their questions. Where museum information is complex, or where its language is difficult, learners need ways to keep track of what they have experienced in their own words. In public spaces, learners need situations that encourage language, writing, self-presentation, and conversation. They deserve significant settings for the pursuit of the unfinished inquiries that occur and increase in a contemporary life. They need places to experience the continuities of human knowledge and thought and to sense themselves at the center of the thinking world they occupy.

Provocative questions, alone or in clusters, lead the learner on and may confer order and power as they proceed. The occasion can also bring to mind past models or teachers of influence, enduring relationships with mentors, ethnic and family circles, or other binding influences that touch and inform one life. These memories may be inexpressible, but they are no less moving forces in the museum, attuning the sensitivities of the learner to resonant moments. A question or conversation is remembered; a recommended book or article is recollected; a film or documentary comes to mind. In the design of a learning life, there is an invisible history enacting its influence, tempering the connections and patterns the learner forges, and framing both the learner's image of the world and the learner's questions about how that world works.

Support for the Learner

An educative museum will assume that its users are present in order to know something or to construct a new experience for themselves. It must attend to questions and uncertainties, the unknowns of strangers. The responsive museum will strive to understand the interests and inquiries of learners whose voices will never otherwise be heard directly by museum planners and administrators. Lives deepen when they are expressed, heard, and understood by others. The museum that intends to cause deepening and quickening of minds, that hopes to transform the casual visitor into a thoughtful learner, will offer primary support for the processes of inquiry. Some possibilities follow.

Pervasive information. An educative museum is an informing environment, a structure of knowledge designed for discovery. Information here is used to mean knowledge capable of being described and transmitted between minds—including some messages that have no words, like awe or mystery. On a practical level, quotations, excerpts from written works, bibliographic citations, allusions to recent relevant events, or statements of curatorial reasoning will begin to provide an informing environment. A collection of information tools might be nearby, especially atlases, handbooks, and encyclopedias. An educative museum provides the opportunity to grasp information, guided by suggestions of pattern, order, continuity, and the pervasive logics of its own structure. Even if it is tacit, the informing logic of the educative museum is always present—inherent in texts and identifications, directions, signs, and references—and capable of reconstruction by its users.

Definitive texts. Occasions for language in a museum are limitless; inevitably they will lead to further occasions for talk and perhaps writing. Some texts are obvious: organizing terms and narratives appear on labels and signs, in accompanying brochures and audio texts, in the narratives of interpreters, and in material available in the museum library and store. Their purpose is to support and deepen the sensory experiences at hand. Thoughtful museums also might refer a user to standard texts or suggest adaptable handbooks and scholarly guides, published in the museum or elsewhere.

Knowledge structures. Every museum presents itself as a structure holding organized knowledge. Beyond available language, the sequences, juxtapositions, and densities of museum exhibitions also inform the museum user's experience. In some places, ambient qualities of illumination, fragrance, and sound inform the user, as do other senses, such as touch. Experiences are informed by what the museum requires its users to do and by what it gives them an opportunity to express. Maps, directories, and even the crowding among the Impressionism galleries inform the user about what the museum experience means. Labels can be systematically structured to describe origins and contexts, exemplary qualities of the evidence, and its place within the larger academic, cultural, or scientific frame. Scholars and commentators can be cited, linking the museum to its disciplines and thinkers; bookstores and libraries can fulfill these connections.

Living connections. The educative museum offers knowledge connected to lived lives, especially the lived lives of the museum's present users. The most evident embodiment of this connection appears in the voices of living humans—researchers, inquirers, artists, explorers, writers, and witnesses—who express the possibility that the museum's collections or exhibitions are important sources for personal development now and in the future. Museums and their amassed collections can inspire inexplicable feelings or intimations of obscure secrets. Masterworks generate mysteries and evoke unknowns over distance and time. What can be done with these alluring thoughts? Where awe, mystery, or ambiguity separate the user from the object, a human observer, expressing gently guiding questions, may permit tentative thoughts to expand.

Individual control. An educative museum demonstrates that it is possible and valuable to design experiences for learning in museums. The museum encourages its users to approach the museum as an opportunity to select specific experiences, to spend time proportionally, and to think of the moment as an occasion with focus and purpose. Toward this end, an educative museum can encourage basic ways to learn in the museum. For example,

- Use the museum with a tentative plan in mind, allowing open time for unexpected discoveries.

- Document museum experiences with a camera or notebook.

- Bring a companion for conversations and informal dialogues.

- Learn to "read" the museum's objects consistently, comparing origins, contexts, implications, or personal responses.

- Carry a relevant handbook or other text.

- Seek key information in labels; read labels for specific information.

- After an hour in the museum, revisit the tentative plan; change it as needed.

- Think and talk about your experiences beyond the museum.

- Use other cultural institutions with similar and supportive collections.

- Explore libraries with your museum experiences in mind.

- Before you leave, plan a return to the museum with new intentions.

Behind these suggestions is the message that it is possible to think of oneself as a serious inquirer in the museum, much as one thinks of oneself while solving an elusive reference problem in a library. Further, these ideas assume a second use, and more.

Free inquiry. Like the library, an educative museum expands experiences and explores boundaries without risk to the user of censure or failure. The user's experiences are private, and the authority of the museum, unlike the authority of the school, is derived from the integrity of its content and its presentation, not from its curriculum, nor from the evaluative power of teachers, mediators, or administrators. The challenge of the object and the experience prevail, unmitigated and uncompromised.

Connection. Perhaps the purpose of all cultural institutions is the revelation of generative connections between ourselves and the world; an object leads to ideas, to further observations, to additional similar objects, and to the thriving buzz outside the museum or inside our heads. No other institutions extend so freely, so independently from authority, or with such openness to individual interpretation. Whatever the museum user's thoughts, the museum is convivial and expansive. It confirms the mind's free play, connects it to a future, and constructs new limits.

Multiple paths. An educative museum acknowledges and supports the idea that multiple ways and levels of exploration are possible, and that variations of approach and process can be explored. Museum experiences fit the user's current interests, previous knowledge, and desired depth; no single pattern of approach is required. Multiple levels of engagement—from naive observations to deep, authentic dialogue between connoisseurs—can be encouraged with simple stimuli. By assisting the user to arrive at a fitting process, the museum defines itself as an educator, an instrumental agency where learning and the learner are valued.

Resource and forum. The rarest achievements of an educative museum are the steps it takes to go beyond the collection of objects and texts, to become a forum for the voices and experiences of learners. An educative museum can create such an environment by setting aside a physical space and time within the museum for interaction and moderated discourse among users. The concept of the museum-as-forum acknowledges that the museum experience is a cognitive immersion, an experiment with depth and density, consisting of stimulating and masterful artifacts, and scholarly knowledge of natural and constructed worlds. The forum acknowledges that the human experience of these things will fill the mind, that human experiences and human language are inextricably linked, and that unexpressed insights are often lost, even to their author. An educative museum finds its greatest powers, first, in helping the user to see and understand, and second, to break through silence and express to others what these perceptions might mean.

A Museum User's Skills

An immersion in the museum can be understood as a problem for the museum user. Is there an arrangement of objects to be understood? Are there optimal ways to see this arrangement? Does the museum capture something whole, or does it hold only fragments? What's missing? How does a person grasp the whole story, beyond the museum's limited view? The idea of *museum use* as a set of various skills can be understood as a way to construct meanings in response to such questions.

Museum use as a skill set recognizes that the cultural institution is a different cognitive environment from any other; it is not the school, the home, or the workplace. Its contents, by definition, are extraordinary; the circumstances for experience and information are unusually rich; the concentration of meanings it suggests is intense. The human being who enters these circumstances needs to manage and control the process.

The museum user *uses* the environment to see and compare objects directly, to understand their differences, and to think about them in relation to a lived life. The museum holds evidence in one place, to be observed and then recollected in the subsequent intellectual life of the observer. Consequently, modeling the following skills of museum use are important investments for every museum, to be kept in mind against the undertow of distractions in a life outside the museum.

> *Understanding the frame.* The user needs to grasp the museum's mission, its scope and immediate aims. The user also needs to understand the premises and assumptions organizing the institution and its themes. An anthropologist's museum is different from an archaeologist's museum, and both of these museums will differ from an art historian's or a connoisseur's museum, though the same objects may be collected in each.
>
> *Using language.* An educative museum supports the user's ability to frame an experience in words—in observations, questions, or speculations. Through initial language a learner comes to understand the larger and more complex

aims that lie in the future. Language reduces mystery and awe; it gives power; it is an ancillary to critical thinking. Users need language to name and organize their experiences, to plan, and to communicate with companions. Though we may lack enough words to express the complexities of museum experience fully to others, we are at a loss if we remain silent to ourselves.

Articulating questions. What questions fit within the frameworks and collections of the museum? What themes move through the various parts of the collection? What is the most productive way to compare objects? What might I consider more deeply among these objects? What might I learn from other observers? How might I find out more? The skill implied in articulating questions means that the question can be asked repeatedly with no loss of meaning, though the contexts of the collections may differ. A good question remains unanswerable in full and continually recurs.

Discovering objects. Every object bears characteristics and implications; every object holds meanings; but because its origins are distant, the restoration of an appropriate context is a difficult challenge. An educative museum will offer information on the origins of an object, its place among other objects of a similar kind, its rarity or illustrative qualities, the contribution it makes to knowledge, details that offer insights, and critical or historical perspectives in the voices of scholars, peers, or a person uniquely qualified to speak (a scientist, an artist, a poet, a musician). What is the story of this piece? What information is evident in the thing itself? What historical or critical knowledge surrounds the object? Where might it fit in the world outside the museum? Even if this heuristic is used sparingly, the questioner is likely to be drawn into the details of the collection.

Understanding contexts. Objects are embedded in time, geography, provenance, event, innovation, or theme. A single piece may have been the catalyst for a revolution in technique, vision, or possibility. A specimen is placed in its taxonomy; an example is placed within its type. How many other kinds of context might there be? Form, function, origin, influence; a piece may be an exemplar of mastery, or a representative of the everyday. Social or disciplinary contexts may surround an object as well: politics, anthropology, warfare, religion, belief systems, human relationships, the discovery or creation processes—they are limitless. A museum that uses only one context (art history, say) to explain objects with vast cultural implications disempowers the museum user.

Thinking critically. It is possible for an educative museum to offer its users models for critical thinking in applied situations. Explanations can demonstrate the comparative and connective thinking, evaluation of evidence, and attention to detail that characterizes critical thought. The museum array can lead to contrasts that illuminate differences; it can create problems by juxtaposing evidence, and it can assist users to understand and act in situations where judging and evaluating follow naturally from observing. Over time, an educative museum can develop repeated opportunities for its users to make tentative judgments, to see these judgments compared to the experiences of others, and to revise them as new insights occur.

Thinking personally. Every adult museum user bears traces of the past and revisits these in the course of museum inquiry. Conversations and questions that lead the user into these memories are important processes in an educative museum. Reaching for insights among the resources of the self assists the user to recognize the use and value of past knowledge; it can help to recover and address old beliefs and revise past miseducation. In the museum, the learner is on an individual, independent course where transforming ideas follow from personal recognitions; these ideas cannot be given to a surrogate, nor can a teacher artificially impart them.

Going beyond. Pursuing an interest beyond the museum, an inspired learner can use libraries, local experts, the World Wide Web, other collections, and national organizations.

Information tools and bibliographic citations help learners to consider a new move toward inquiry. The educative museum engenders learning with a future.

Even encyclopedic museums cannot fully resolve all of the tensions and ambiguities of human inquirers, but all museums can alter and transform, slightly or gently, what its users know by grounding new knowledge, information, and imaginative experiences in immediate observations and objects. An educative museum of any size helps its users to go beyond itself, and to go beyond themselves as well, by suggesting possibilities of thought and then offering the means to explore them. An educative museum nurtures the transformation of unformed, unspoken questions into continuing, self-directed inquiries. This transformation matters deeply to learning, because it causes the museum user to enter a territory where thinking constructs the path.

Living Up to the User

As instruments for informing and changing the cognitive lives of users, educative museums inspire knowledge that is tentative and possible, as well as knowledge that is confirmed. This is what we know now, it says. What new knowledge has become possible for you here? What possibilities or new ways of thought have been evoked? The best acts and designs of these museums ought to inspire a future of museum use by presenting information and offering the user some control over an intellectual domain. Acting for the future rests on the capacity of museum leaders to envision the needs of people in both the museum's collections and the living worlds outside them.

Without and within the museum, human beings bear memories and harbor privacies; they ask questions, examine situations, wonder aloud; they seek readings, look for people who can help, and think seriously about new information. In the educative museum, these fragments of an inquiring life can find form; given form, the inquiring life has a future.

Museum encounters happen best where the situations and constraints of users are considered, where minds are no less precious than objects, and where the challenges of planning, trying out, and evaluating have been undertaken.

An educative museum lives up to its users when it unlocks its own structure. It describes potential paths toward a whole view, or toward new information. It contains places for reflection and opportunities to hold a thought—and it helps to create the need for similar places and activities in the user's life beyond the museum.

In the following agenda I list the ways an educative museum works to create responsive, reflective, and observant people, each with a memory and a future, for whom museum use is a process of and for the evolving mind. The goals of such museums are to:

> *Evoke individual responses.* Educative practice will undermine anonymity by constructing situations that cause users to make choices, encounter ambiguities and remember themselves as mature learners. Whether these situations are brought about by memory, laughter, or confusion does not matter; they express the museum as a place of self-presentation, beyond the everyday.
>
> *Define the museum as an information provider.* An educative museum will recognize that information stimulates people, attracts and evokes interest, and causes people to think and thrive. This museum will also be sensitive to the adaptations, concentrations of attention, and struggles with the past that move people into adulthood. Maturity seems to require that our lives must be rethought and reordered, and we are often given much confusion to advance this task. Cultural institutions exist to feed the mature hunger for information and to nurture the capacity to ask questions, evaluate data, and interpret our lived experiences.
>
> *Present a heuristic.* Every museum presents evidence as a kind of problem, and can assist the learner's desire to understand through questions. What has been brought here?

How are these objects organized and described? What knowledge helps to explain their origins? What connections might be made to other experiences available here? What words describe what I have experienced? Naive questions unlock complexities. They lead to others; they provide a bare context for grasping the experience of the museum; they open the possibility of less neutral and more formative inquiries.

Think with the user. We are always challenged to understand other minds, to spend time with people who wish to learn, and to sense the patterns of attention, memory, and aspiration that move them. Support for museum users should reflect an informed, vivid awareness of others, respect for any person's experience as an original path, and the knowledge that all lives contain unfinished issues.

Address the future. The best museum learning leaves the museum, in the mind and conversation of the learner. It occurs in the days following a museum visit. No museum can control these future effects, but it can strive to create situations of lasting coherence and impact. The satisfactions of engaged thoughts and stimulating interpretations are continuous. No learner wishes to lose a strong experience or allow its lessons to fade; the museum can help to construct the critical second use by inviting the user to return for unexplored connections, forthcoming lectures, and new exhibitions on similar themes. The museum is an invitational institution; there are many ways to invite the learner.

Regardless of its size or content, the educative museum is an infinitely variable space, where users may create many paths. They can recover divergent memories in response to the same stimulus, or they can find a common illuminating insight from divergent experiences. An individual user will experience many strands of meaning in the educative museum; there is no single story, nor one inflexible path to select. The educative museum will harbor alternative ways to think about the world, and offer many opportunities to reorganize experience, find a new angle, and when needed, begin again.

Any educator knows how difficult it is to live up to the learner, and how difficult it is to create lasting encounters with ideas. If museums are to assist their users to explore and develop what they know, they must invite the avalanche of questions and create the webwork of connections that configure a learning life. In this way, the museum can become a forum for people who wish to know, understand, and communicate about the complexities of experience. There are few resources for such learners, few places to practice reflective observation, and even fewer places to talk to others.

An educative museum exists for those learners who seek new information in a changing world, who find value in new encounters that revise old knowledge, and who hope to reweave the fabric of what they know. A museum that assists these processes invites the learner, consistently and intentionally, to participate in the surprises, possibilities, and delights of thoughtful change.

Note

1. Unfortunately, the encyclopedia for which this entry has been prepared does not yet exist.

3

In the Contexts of the Possible: Libraries and Museums as Incendiary Cultural Institutions

I

Great cultural institutions—incendiary cultural institutions—feed flames that illuminate the human capacity to imagine the possible.

When we consider our institutions as dramatic stages or as provocative forums—places where human beings present themselves to each other, act to change their cognitive lives, perform the passions of their searches, frame their hopeful inquiries, tentatively assert their aspirations—we begin to understand that we contemplate and preside over a place where something essential and revolutionary goes on. But what situations for learning could live up to the metaphor of flame and fire? What would such an institution be? How might an incendiary cultural institution think of itself?

Whenever we speak about the library and the museum, and whenever we consider the power of institutions to address and respect the integrity of human intellect and human becoming, the incendiary minds and watchful eyes of Thomas Jefferson and James Madison are in the room. So are the minds and eyes of our communities and our cultures, those who live and grow strong in our civil societies, families, and schools—all await, contemplating the challenges of their lives, hoping to be addressed and assisted in the course of their own individual human becoming.

When people come together as learners under the aegis of a library or museum, they have an opportunity to understand that cultural institutions—libraries, museums, historical societies, botanical gardens, archives, zoos, parks—are grounded in the idea that a culture requires places, forums, working laboratories for cognitive change, where voices can be heard expressing hopes and aspirations in the contexts of the possible. When we capture and express such possibilities, we come to own a view of the future. In such places—truly open sources of our society—there is also equality in those possibilities of ownership, assuring that knowledge is not privileged to any but those who can learn from the records and objects at hand and from other people in mutual engagement with a common world.

In this coming together we find our several challenges: *Overcoming the isolations of experience*, our separations and insularities, the anxieties and distances among us. *Creating the language of observation*, exploration, and common exchange. *Building accord on what we want to have happen*, deciding what we want our institutions to do and be. *Finding the courage* to consider a mutually shared, possibly intimidating unknown.

This is exactly why cultural institutions exist: to manage our cognitive challenges by creating good processes and educative structures, to recognize and celebrate good questions when they appear, and to engage with the personal narratives of human beings as they learn through responding to those questions.

And yet, the "personal" has become increasingly elusive, as our connections and transactions become increasingly virtual; they have become increasingly transient as well. As we negotiate our way to the learning structures we need, we may feel that something of our own is missing, or it may be lost in the tensions that define our lives: tensions between our families and our work, between feeling safe and feeling fearful, the indeterminate tensions between continuity and change. These are all tensions of knowledge, discrepancies between what we know and what we do not yet know, the hopes of having enough information to manage a complex life with extraordinary unknowns in it.

To these tensions, we might add the observation that the values that define our lives, inform our educational systems, and are transmitted to our children may not be coming from us, but from somewhere outside us. Where, then, do they begin, and how do they reach us and shape our environments? These are times when the unresolvable tacit questions we are asked to live with may be, What does it mean to be a human being? What are the values of a person—and of personal acts? What does it mean now to be a human being among other human beings?

We who are advocates for cultural institutions as sources of structure, continuity, and transformation may be sensitive to less identifiable, even more subtle erosions in public altruism. In our own lives, we may notice fewer opportunities for reflection and self-renewal, more difficult connections to others, an inability to find a common voice. In our work, we may experience less cooperation and outreach, less mutual respect, less self-respect. These erosions are especially important to us, of course, because they affect the grounding impulses for teaching, learning, self-exploration, and confident engagement with one's life. To lose them, even a bit of them, is disheartening, so we must seize what we have.

In a poem, "Utterance," by W. S. Merwin, the poet, "Sitting over words / very late," hears

> a kind of whispered sighing
> not far
> like a night wind in pines or like the sea in the dark
> the echo of everything that has ever
> been spoken . . .[1]

Against the "the echo of everything that has ever been spoken," the tensions and senses of loss, we take the life we have, we create communities of all kinds, and we build harbors in them: the institutions and collective settings where commonalities and stories and the mutual transmissions of cultural gifts are exchanged. These are the institutions and settings doing the formative cultural mediation that is the practical work of civil society,[2] the ways a community has of causing or encouraging favorable things to happen.[3]

In libraries and museums, the favorable thing we want to have happen is the development of learners, alone and in groups and families, whose lives are engaged with each other—embracing each other over their mutual reflections. For us, it is also the confirmation of observers, readers, and thinkers, nourishing and encouraging them to experience and synthesize new information. That critical work is the setting of minds on fire in such a way that they inch their edges forward, toward new knowledge and toward each other. Jean Bethke Elshtain writes, "Civil society isn't so much about problem solving as about citizen and neighbor creating."[4] And learner creating, I will add, and memory creating, and future creating. As Dan Coats and Rick Santorum write, "When civil society is strong, it infuses a community with its warmth, trains its people to be good citizens, and transmits values between generations."[5] To me, this is what our cultural institutions must be about, and what we who work in them must be for.

Certainly, it is what we at our best do better than anyone else. We find the energy of people who arrive in the library, the garden, the museum, or the zoo in order to renew and reinvent themselves, and so to renew and reinvent their awareness of the culture they inhabit and own. Our cultural institutions recognize that every mindful person is a community's treasure. To serve in such institutions is to exist in an alliance of trust and common weal with a community. The preposition is important: it is the institution that is not just *for*, but *with* its community in trust, that thrives most fully.[6]

II

How are cultural institutions part of common human motives, beyond the fundamental idea of keeping things and preserving them against the threat of loss and forgetfulness? Having a museum and a library in a community is always about the community having an informed present and future. These institutions are devoted to the unknown, and to the evidences of possible knowledge, constructed on the foundations of the known.

- Cultural institutions share a horizon, attending to the cognitive, educative, and developmental possibilities of people over their lifespans, apart from the interests and expectations of schools. They don't give credits or certificates. They don't graduate anyone. No bells. No recess. But they are for learning as it perhaps ought to happen best, in what we might call an open configuration of structures and structures-within-structures, evoking the natural continuities of cognitive experience.

- They have similar logics and patterns of organization: While we may be challenged as independent observers, we can expect to find our ways in museums and libraries with reasonable amounts of attention and minimal intervention and instruction. Every public cultural setting in my experience is constructed for direct, independent entry by users, who are typically given articulate, logical, public organization systems and coherent narratives for passage or process. Each institution employs professionals and others whose specific task is to consult, direct, facilitate learning, and assist the user in designing an individual experience of the collection. Apart from the more or less logical systems created for access (such as catalogs and maps), the physical structures of museum and library buildings generally reflect a logical likeness or design, a continuity of discipline, topic, or material. The museum and the library are designed structures, with a logic that is, at its best, visible and coherent, unhidden, unmysterious. A setting that evokes a path that we can experience as our own path.

- In what they offer and how they offer it to us, the museum and the library are similarly laboratory-like environments: in content and power, they are potentially volatile and surprising, and they require acute attention to detail. Borrowing from John Dewey, we might say that museums and libraries are places for events that have not happened yet. Our cultural institutions are, by their nature, designed for cognitive experiments, for proximities and juxtapositions of images and ideas that cannot occur in any other institutions. And, in library or museum, every user's step is a form of question, from generic to specific. Because library and museum use are active and experimental, not passive, we might further say that such experiences are empirical, revealing logical connections and decisions that require direct cognitive impressions of artifacts and tools. Holding these artifacts and tools for us, they are places where our hand-made lives, our crafted truths, are shaped.

- Both museum and library, even those with limited collections and services, are engaged in organizing provocative and complex realms of knowledge that exist parallel to corresponding experiential worlds outside. Both institutions must forge illuminating links to the world beyond their walls. They are culturally charged in the connections they make to situations and settings beyond the institutions themselves. The museum and library are, in fact, dependent on the world outside; each place is a treasury that is renewed in value by the progress of its exterior cultures. As institutions, they are complex in their potential interactions with their communities, and with each other. It is also clear that libraries and museums never become simpler; the complexity of their content never grows less.

- In museum or library, nothing moves forward without a question, pursuit or an objective, a mix of risk and hope. Even casual use of a cultural institution typically takes on an aim or plan within the limits of time, interest, or skill. It follows from the need to find something, even if invisible or inexplicable. Purposeful use in both institutions might be described in searching language: I am looking for ———, I want to see ———, I am trying to find ———. Museum and library need to cultivate and follow the multiple forms of a searching sensibility.

- Museum and library integrate past and present, embodied in the user. A thoughtful person in the museum or library brings a history of knowing, reflecting, and understanding to bear on the moment of use and the design of the search at hand. In the learner's intellectual processes, everything discovered is compared to past experiences and previous knowledge. (Of course, that person also carries a history of confusion, questioning, and mystery.) Not only does a user encounter the new and the historic, the user also encounters the past that is carried within, as well as an emerging new idea. The here and now blends its dimensions with the once and the past. No other institutions require us to travel in so many private dimensions of time and space at once.

- Wherever inquiry takes place, literacy guides the discoveries of the user. Language assists the user to find the way toward information, and to understand and process information. The critical intellectual factors of explanation, articulation, and synthesis are experiences of language. Without words, and a level of fluency, we cannot articulate, in public or private, what has happened in the presence of a work, an idea, an object, a text. Because we have words, we have the ability to capture and then to hold and contain what we witness.

- We can work and think in these institutions for as long as we live. Only the library and the museum, among institutions for learning, allow multiple generations to reflect side by side. This means that the interests of an individual, across his or her lifespan can be explored and renewed over time, transmitted to others, and never be exhausted from youth to old age. It also means that youths and elders can gather to tell the stories stimulated by words and things. In museums and libraries, age, knowledge, family, educational, or economic status are not barriers to use. Perhaps it is time to suggest that formative cultural institutions might construct the lifelong learner far more directly than any classroom.

- And when we enter the cultural institution, we are free within limits to do as we care to do, and free with no limits to think as we care to think. Unlike the school, where the learner must typically submit to the values and interpretations of an instructor, the situation for experience in the cultural institution is largely under the control of the user. Moreover, the institution succeeds *only* when it has responded to the needs of the individual user. The responsive institution makes direct, authentic, and unrestricted experiences possible for the user, then it helps the user illuminate those experiences and see them in further, deeper, richer, more extensive contexts.

- Museum and library succeed through the useful tensions combining intellectual work and intellectual play, the known and the unknown, the conventional and (sometimes right next to it) the revolutionary. When we enter a cultural institution, we find there an environment that challenges and tempts us, even as we find more to know than we can possibly master. For the mindful learner, a single possibility can create a powerful tension between the desirable and the actual, the clear and the shrouded. These are the tensions of learning.

- The structure and process of the museum and the library are the same for every learner: One must begin where one is, assessing the parts of knowledge to be grasped and mastered over time. The learning is connective and integrative, evolving slowly and not arriving as if for an examination. Here, learners fabricate and build their own minds; they do not wait to receive the mind of a professor or other teacher. Here, learners combine pieces for themselves. Nothing about this is easy.

- Ultimately, at their core, both museums and libraries are institutions that give information to their users: through vision, words, comparisons, suggestions, or the powerful presence of a reorganizing concept, an insightful connection. Libraries connect information to individual cognitive, personal, imaginative, and economic energies and processes. Museums connect information to the experiences of awe and surprise that follow from seeing the thing itself that has been brought before us.

We are increasingly challenged to understand how these twelve common themes take different forms in museums and libraries, how they might be more explicitly woven together, and how our historic community genius can invigorate the patterns of thought and aspiration that unify their missions. We are challenged to understand what these two institutions might become, together. We are challenged to encounter the idea that cultural institutions have a common agenda and that libraries and museums both hold and construct a powerful vision of inquiry and knowledge in culture.

III

If we agree on some of these common qualities among cultural institutions, we might also consider several fundamental ideas that seem to sustain such institutions in our lives. Why do human beings need these institutions, these collections, this information? What unknowns, wants, and urgencies do they mirror in our hearts and minds? This is an individual perspective on reasons for having museums and libraries, reasons for rescuing, conserving, and sustaining the treasures of culture and identity, and reasons for sharing their conjoint value and power with fellow citizens.

Human beings collect, organize, and keep evidences of their lives and cultures for multiple reasons: for the pleasures of ownership; for personal identification; for the cultivation of knowledge and the advancement of scholarship; for the possibility of change through reflection. We are certain—because we see the events of our own lives and the lives of our ancestors as worthy—that we are obligated to contain and illuminate the artifacts and ideas of persons now gone. Objects of art, memory, identity, or wisdom bear in common the touch of human, caring hands. Their presence in a contemporary world suggests that among their qualities, simple endurance may be worth our attention and reflection. And so: we keep these institutions in order to understand and assure the enduring qualities of a handmade life.

Reasons for keeping and understanding objects and texts, and for explaining their lasting strength, are more than private. They are sources of insight and recognition for the individual, and for other learners in groups. But if we assume that such insight and thought go *with* the user, *beyond* the institution, we must also assume that cultural treasures are alike in that *they are about the future* more than they are about the past. If our record is to be of use, it must be given to the future. The formal institutions we have built to hold the evidences of our civilization and are too often regarded as precious reliquaries or display cases. Instead, they should be seen as formative and interactive, creating whatever is to happen next in the cognitive life of the user. Having a museum or library in a community is about the community having both a present and a future, since these institutions are devoted to exploring the generative possibilities of the evidence at hand.

Across time and geography, our public cultural institutions are grounded in concepts and intentions that we rarely articulate. What are the deepest cultural purposes of cultural institutions? Why do we strive to contain, to keep, and to narrate the documents and artifacts of human knowledge and activity? What do we construct, when we construct a cultural institution? What do we assemble for ourselves when we build a library or a museum?

- We build collections because we strive *to keep and preserve* evidences of human continuity, and in order to sustain remembrance. We strive not to forget how we have become who and what we are, in order to be mindful of where we began. Cultural institutions hold artifacts and their legacies, when our memories as humans cannot. This makes possible the transmission of meanings among distant generations.

- We construct and systematize collections because we strive *to contain and organize* authoritative materials for reference and verification. By looking at the original artifact—the edited manuscript, the sculpted bone, the tortured score—we are nearly able to look at (and into) the moment of its inspiration. By retaining the records of masterful ideas and objects, we keep the possibility of drawing new insights from them. The museum and library allow us the opportunity, generation after generation, to respond separately to the questions, "Is it true? And what, exactly, is its truth?"

- As inquirers, we strive *to discover and study* materials for new knowledge and new syntheses of evidence. Driven by questions, we use our cultural institutions as places where we can first follow threads and then weave garments. If every school were to close tomorrow, intellectual growth might continue in cultural institutions, where we would be likely to find and teach each other. These settings are always poised to rescue human cognitive processes when schools fail to sustain and nurture them and even when the Internet undoes the tendency to have an original, private, unshared thought.

- In museums and libraries, we strive *to delight and inform* ourselves with observations and reflections on human accomplishment. Human beings have always reserved their greatest delights for moments of learning. The parent and the child are bonded as much by the learning transmitted between them as they are by blood. What we find delightful, we wish (like Faust) to have held forever before us, Faustlike. The museum or library does this, while generously allowing us to retain the integrity and ownership of our souls.

- We strive *to integrate and verify* our experiences in the larger culture. Our cultural institutions are mirrors for the people and societies that construct them, naturally. But in each personal discovery or observation, a learner also finds a mirror of lived experience: "I remember an object like this in San Francisco." "The quality of light in this work appears sometimes in Copenhagen." "The evolution of tools fascinates me and leads me on." "My grandparents were once in this part of the world." We enter and leave with what we know, but our knowing is different when we depart the institution because we have clarified, augmented, or revised what knowledge we had. Or what we know is in the process of becoming different knowledge, because we are present, working to understand things. Since what we know configures who we are, we might also say that the crafting of truth in cultural institutions is a process of becoming, renewing, or confirming ourselves.

- We strive *to settle fears* of loss. We seem at times to be particularly haunted by loss, and by the fear of loss. Change, the arrival of strangers, the frequency of feeling discontinuous with the past, the terror of beginning again—all of these advance the sense of eroding integrity in our lives. As the greatest of cultural educators, the cultural institution can make explicit links between our pasts and our futures, drawing us toward an understanding of great, immutable themes. In doing so, it can help us to gain cognitive control over an otherwise unimaginable transition and to place ourselves clearly within our own times, integrated and not excluded. A museum or library collection allows us to revisit and reconsider the differences between what was and what is, and to see ourselves in continuity with the others who have preceded and who will follow us.

If museums and libraries are to recognize their common future and reorganize themselves to address it, generalizations such as those offered in this text will require exploration and reflection, based on strong groundings in empirical observations and educational theory. The individual learner, the family as a learning organism, the process of sense making in the presence of an unknown, the continuities and connections among learners who speak to each other and make their stories, fears, and learnings known—we need to understand these invisible things even more than we need to understand the histories of texts and objects. Museums and libraries have one research agenda that overshadows all others: we need to know more about how individual learners renew themselves by exploring their literacies and possibilities, and we can learn this best by talking directly to people.

The final concept unifying the museum and the library is the idea that all cultural institutions must act on the tenet that *every mindful person is a community's treasure*. As our culture changes, the culture of every institution needs to find new forms of professional thought, grounded in a new cognitive environment. The truly educative institution will experiment with new ideas of professional service to the exploring user. In a world that becomes increasingly virtual, cultural institutions must be challenged to redesign themselves toward becoming face-to-face forums where the questions and controversies of a living culture can find their form and be debated. It is through such forums that human beings experience the realities of democratic cultural literacy and may come to embody the tensions of being both a responsible citizen and a mindful person. There is no country on earth without the need for such forums.

IV

How does the incendiary institution think of itself? It must understand its own energy and how that energy attracts and engages its users: How does it lead people in, involve them with their own choices and with other human beings, help them to understand the structures at hand, and teach them how to move among those structures with eyes open? The incendiary institution never compromises its respect for the open-eyed user.

Such users will increase in number when the institution addresses them and the problems that learning presents to a contemporary life. As people experience the inexorable growth of both the tasks and the information at hand, there will also be a common increase in ambiguity and irresolution. How do we know what we need next? How do we confirm the accuracy or truth of our observations? What does learning in one frame of our lives (as a parent, or as a companion) mean to the learning we carry out in other frames of our lives (as a colleague, a designer of new experiences, an educator of other adults)?

It is a commonplace that receiving and deciding about immense amounts of information increasingly require our time and attention if we are to be appropriately responsive to our world. And yet, our lives then become less our own, because as messages and information increase, the more we must think about the horizons of others, contend with the structures and assumptions of others, and negotiate meaning and think critically in worlds designed or deeply influenced by others.

And so the living challenge to any person is double edged: to live strongly on one's own horizon and yet also adapt our horizons among others in order to find contexts of what we want, what we see, and what we hope for together. No one can meet the challenges of such a life without being a passionately critical thinker, an author of one's own experience, and a cautious master of one's own intellect. In a culture where "knowledge" arrives unbidden instantly, it is problematic to confirm its authority, value, and relevance; we need to question. The design of real, not surrogate, experiences becomes important as we grow increasingly remote from living a self-constructed life; we need ways to determine what is authentic. And when information is unlimited in both speed and density, it is not good for reflection; we need to slow it down and leaven it with our own salient ideas and values.

As I tell my students, our task is to slow down the information revolution. This is also every learner's task.

Reflection is essential for understanding the configuration of the world—the mass of influences that create human experience—and its concomitant tensions, balances, processes, and assumptions. Reflection will always be essential for any person who strives to move forward, toward wholeness against fragmentation, toward integrity against compromise, and toward fearlessness in the presence of things unknown. As ever, learning and reflection will depend on engaging ceaselessly with the processes that configure a cognitive experience: planning, questioning, remembering, pursuing, discovering, evaluating, constructing, and connecting.

When we face our primary task as adults—to arrive at a working sense of identity and integrity—we have no choice other than to do it as learners, led by our own thoughts, and not solely by the thoughts and horizons of others. In cultural institutions, people must always undertake this courageous task against the odds. The mass, the authority, and sometimes the intractability of our institutions require great strength of mind if we are to overcome both brilliance and awe in order to see the small traces of an inspired hand. But even in our mindfulness (and here is one of the tensions that will not go away), we must also be permeable to the living experiences and words of others, feeling safe enough in our own lives to encounter new questions that expand our grasp, even though they may at first make us fearful of change.

Learning will take place as it has always taken place in the contexts of the possible: (1) A human being will create a question in a situation of complexity; (2) that question will stimulate a felt need to pursue information in multiple formats, wherever it may lead; and (3) that information will create more questions, lead to more or less useful information; until (4) the problem, its contexts, what it means to the learner, and an array of possible questions have all become clearer; and (5) for the learner, the first step toward changes in thought, attention, or behavior will also become clear. These are all incendiary moments. They cannot occur without structures and processes, or without a logical system of informing paths. And, of course, they require some spark or match, perhaps, or a bolt from the sky.

These elements must be present in the situation, if learning is to take place:

- *Assistance*, freely given by a mentor, a model, a source of information or referral, a person who speaks the language of the learner; and *access* to this person, meaning opportunities to create questions and develop a relationship

- *Tools*, a broad array of adaptive and generative, convivial tools (the term is Ivan Illich's)—tools that suggest syntheses, ideas for recombination and exploration, tools that lead a learner on, stimulating new responses to experience, tools that assist the user to transfer skills and observations to another place and time

- *Autonomy,* meaning independence from authority, freedom from any evaluation other than meeting the learner's own satisfaction, freedom to accept or reject a mentor

- *Control* and *authorship* of an inquiry—for example, frequent opportunities to revise the themes and patterns of an inquiry, or to abandon it altogether

- A *forum* or a *conversation* in an open environment where learners can participate in mutual conversations with other learners

People come to the museum and to the library, and they look to it as a place to hold things still, as the world has fewer and fewer places of stillness in it. That is a critical thing to do. And yet, at the same moment it offers stillness in a turning world, the great cultural institution must also understand itself to be *challenging,* a *creator* of learners and thinkers, a setting where mindfulness cannot possibly be abjured. For any learner, of any age, the great library, the great museum, must be an advocate for new thinking, based on the astonishing, moving evidence in treasured texts and objects. Only the place that has a heart of fire (and not of ice) is the place where learning can happen best.

Sustenance for the mind of the future will come from excellent information near at hand, as it always has; but it will also come from collaboration among human beings, in an alliance for knowledge, identity, and mere connection to another person—as it always has. Every day of service in a cultural institution provides an opportunity to reinvent the idea of a helping mind, to reconfigure a repertoire of ideas and tools, and to construct connections to whatever might happen next. We may slowly come to understand that every life bears its own unfinished issues, and every life is unfinished in a different way. In a world often characterized by loss and fear, certain acts of human rescue and survival can occur only in the places where a culture continuously transforms itself through human associations, forged in the presence of the unknown. In this way, the constructive cultural institution contributes to the integrity of its culture.

Our questions—like telescopes or microscopes—are instruments that concentrate our attention and allow us to focus on those parts of the unknown that engage us most. Without such mechanisms, we cannot understand the dimensions hidden from our vision. Whenever we come together to engage in such conversations, we have made a place that is, of course, full of questions itself, and these questions do not become fewer as an evening wears on. And so we must arrive at last at what may be the best question of all, left here for others to consider through the arts of practice and the human gifts of reciprocity and mutual engagement: What happens when caring minds meet? It is with this question that the incendiary cultural institution must regard itself.

Notes

This essay was published in a slightly different form in *RBM: A Journal of Rare Books, Manuscripts and Cultural Heritage* [Association of College and Research Libraries], 1, no. 2 (2000): 117–135.

1. W. S. Merwin, "Utterance," in *The Rain in the Trees*, ed. Czeslaw Milosz (New York: Knopf, 1988), 44.

2. Former senator Bill Bradley defines civil society this way:

Civil society is the place where Americans make their home, sustain their marriages, raise their families, hang out with their friends, meet their neighbors, educate their children, worship their god. It is in the churches, schools, fraternities, community centers, labor unions, synagogues, sports leagues, PTAs, libraries and barbershops. It is where opinions are expressed and refined, where views are exchanged and agreements made, where a sense of common purpose and consensus are forged. It lies apart from the realms of the market and the government, and possesses a different ethic. The market is governed by the logic of economic self-interest, while government is the domain of laws with all their coercive authority. Civil society, on the other hand, is the sphere of our most basic humanity—the personal, everyday realm that is governed by values such as responsibility, trust, fraternity, solidarity, and love. In a democratic civil society such as ours, we also put a special premium on social equality—the conviction that men and women should be measured by the quality of their character and not the color of their skin, the shape of their eyes, the size of their bank account, the religion of their family, or the happenstance of their gender. [Bill Bradley, "America's Challenge: Revitalizing Our National Community," in E. J. Dionne, Jr., *Community Works: The Revival of Civil Society in America*, E. J. Dionne, Jr., ed. (Washington, D.C.: Brookings Institution Press, 1998), 108–109]

3. Dionne, *Community Works*, 3.

4. Jean Bethke Elshtain, "Not a Cure-All: Civil Society Creates Citizens, It Does Not Solve Problems," in Dionne, *Community Works*, 27.

5. Dan Coats and Rick Santorum, "Civil Society and the Humble Role of Government," in Dionne, *Community Works*, 102.

6. I am grateful to the Children's Museum of Indianapolis for this awareness of prepositions and for much more.

4

A Community Mind

Assume this fragile premise: our best cultural institutions assist in the design and construction of individual lives. We are shaped by what we see and feel. This premise yields another: our best experiences in cultural institutions are formative, providing sudden understandings or questionings; breakthroughs, like uncovered secrets or privacies. Working at our best in libraries and museums, we find implications, imperatives, and possibilities. We are always moving inward, toward our depths. Whatever we may see in the visible world in libraries, museums, and botanical gardens, it is the *in*visible one that holds us rapt, transfixed, and openmouthed, seized in the presence of the mysterious and suggestive. We can barely describe this unusual experience. When we are held in this way, we are engaged by the play of something that is always just about to happen to us.

Assume once more that these invisible actions occur differently for each person, and that, belonging to our interior lives, they affect our feelings and aspirations. We know them to be important, but we can barely sense these invisible moments of promise, and we can scarcely trace the strands and patterns that mark our learning. No matter that museums and libraries—our cultural institutions—offer deep and implicit opportunities for their users to become different human beings. Our encounters with the indelible fingerprints still marking human words and objects are private; the lost voices and the faces waiting just a light breath away from human records are evanescent. We are always learners whose eyes inevitably lead us toward things we cannot see. And yet we know they were made by human hands and minds like ours.

Human communities, visible and invisible, past and present, are embedded in cultural institutions. The best professional thinking in museums and libraries is done with awareness of these invisible actions and unspoken connections. Like the best teachers, we act hopefully to inspire reflection. We build spaces for knowledge to emerge as the outcome of design and structure. We know well that in cultural institutions learners change in all the measures that matter: their aspirations, their senses of continuity, and their willingness to look, however briefly, for the illumination of the unknown. We wait for that moment of illumination, and we design our institutions for it. It is no accident that the library and the museum are among the most purposeful and intentional of institutions. When they are fully given resources and the voices of a responsive, professional, and helping staff, cultural institutions compose the purposeful intelligence of their society, holding the culture's memory and minding its continuing community.

The existence of a library or archive, museum, zoo or garden, a restoration, or even a public memorial assumes these themes as guiding ideas.

- For its duration, every life remains an unfinished system, because its formative texts and situations, and the culture it inhabits, constantly change. This unfinished system remains as long as we live convivially open to new possibilities and new explanations, depending on the breadth or narrowness of our lives, experiences, and hopes. Encounters with the past, with memory, and with new ideas are moments when a metaphorical page may be turned. A good life, like a good theory, remains dynamic and constructive until it can no longer move forward, or has no more promise.

- As the complexities of human lives increase, the powerful undertow of mindless response increases as well. New thoughts are needed to stimulate engagement and capability. Consequently, people must develop and intensify their cognitive strengths in order to swim against that undertow. People must be challenged to remember themselves. Their inner, contemplative lives need grounding in the physical world, in new ideas and experiences, and in a rich language that sustains memory against loss.

- Our collections are not only for capturing and holding the culture at hand, they are also structures designed to enable individuals (in Jerome Bruner's idea) to renegotiate the culture at hand, to allow its steadily evolving complexities to recede, and to recover the power of personal strengths against thoughtlessness.

- Our task is to rescue the user, to enable the broadest and deepest thinking, the kind of thinking that allows us all to go beyond the institution as we know it, and to go beyond ourselves as we know ourselves. And to go beyond our educations, and to go beyond every other limit set on us by others.

- All lives need stories near at hand, and our experiences of narratives in contextually rich worlds are transformative.

Unless an individual life has multiple opportunities to be rescued from banality and to be thoughtfully transformed by a library or a museum or a botanical garden or a planetarium—that is, by a collection of knowledge and experience, passionately gathered and thoughtfully constructed—an important failure of attention has occurred. Our libraries and museums should be intentionally committed, dedicated by mission and service, to the construction of thinking lives, and to the illumination of thoughtful possibilities for those lives. These places are destined to be active and responsive forums, communicative institutions, not passive or reticent. A great cultural institution is a place of friction, heat, light, warmth, and the occasional flame.

A community will be engaged by its cultures only if it is a community where memory resides, where the possibilities and satisfactions of learning are present and valued, and where the future is held not only in its families, churches, and schools, but also in its understandings of the past, wherever that past occurred: in businesses, in public offices, in classrooms and hospitals, on farms and in pulpits, in clubs, in mills and factories, on wilderness trails, in train and bus stations.

Robert N. Bellah and his associates introduce *The Good Society* under this title: "We Live Through Institutions."

> Americans often think of individuals pitted against institutions. It is hard for us to think of institutions as affording the necessary context within which we become individuals; of institutions as not just restraining but enabling us; of institutions not as an arena of hostility within which our character is tested but an indispensable source from which character is formed. This is in part because some of our institutions have indeed grown out of control and beyond our comprehension. But the answer is to change them, for it is illusory to imagine that we can escape them.[1]

The primary source of the cynicism and distrust Bellah describes as a characteristic of our relationships to institutions follows from our terribly prolonged exposure to schooling, an exposure so pervasive that each of us needs to overcome it in his or her own ways. However, by the time we are powerful enough to undo it, aspects of our schooling have done their damage. Over time, we are formed by our early schools, we learn our literacies, find our favorite stories, and perhaps come to understand our own capabilities. But our formative early education seems to thrive on linear progress, external controls, public evaluation, open competition, and humbling self-consciousness. Through these things we often give away our possibilities of personal inquiry and curiosity. As a culture we tend to confound learning with school.

What does this mean for cultural institutions? It is reasonable to describe American culture as one where citizens are systematically taught by schools to assume that the connections among learning and competition, learning and rules, learning and evaluation, and learning and vulnerability are permanent. In schools we are likely to understand that, whatever learning is, it is probably not the constructive, connective, personal, or illuminating process it will become as our lives grow rich with interests and information. It rarely offers us lifelong tools to use against entropy and undertow. We are most often pupils in schools, and too rarely apprentices in exploration and thought.

When our culture allows us to put aside this shallow field of routine, we might find that, in its libraries, museums, and archives, the authentic personal values and questions that define a living culture prevail. In our cultural settings, unlike our schools (including universities), we encourage the learner's solitary, deep immersion in a private, lived experience. We value what no one else can see, and we trust the learner to become the source of order, synthesis, and construction that a good learner can at best become.

Cultural institutions are only in part places dedicated to the capture and control of knowledge and objects; they might more usefully be understood not as places at all, but as the evanescent, constructive moments they contain. We need to understand that libraries, museums, and archives also hold voices, insights, processes, and, in their surprising discoveries, possibilities of mind. We need to understand the work of our cultural institutions as *minding* the community. Perhaps it is less useful to understand cultural institutions as displays of artifacts or constructions of past lives than it is to understand them as the unspoken, continuous, unfinished parts of ourselves, and the mindful emblems of our communal intellectual strengths.

There is a lesson in how Ivan Karp describes the perspective of the African American museum leader Edmund Barry Gaither, who

> envisions museums as crucibles for forging citizens who see themselves as part of civil society, as important members of a

valid social order. Museums have the responsibility to com-
pensate for the failure of other institutions, such as schools, to
show members of minority groups their stake in society. Museums can play this role because they are spaces for the play of
identities, and the multiple natures of those identities can be
made part of museums' exhibitions and programs.[2]

In an essay about multiple kinds of literacies, Lauren Resnick
makes clear that it is not merely the knowing how to read that
matters, but the knowing how to engage in the cultural practices
for which literacy is the key.[3] Cultural institutions are those
places where an ethos of literacy—the telling of lasting stories,
the connecting of objects to realities of past and present, grasping the relationships between knowledge and civic participation,
the understanding of work and craft—can best be realized, far
beyond the limits of our deeply challenged schools. Our greatest
illiteracy, we might say—other than not knowing how to read
our experiences as they evolve—lies in not knowing how to
read the signs of, and participate fully in, the countless cultures
where our lives are forged.

Cultural institutions offer connections to three kinds of engagement that might usefully be considered life-skills. The *first*
of these is involvement with story, meaning the creation of narrative for sorting and constructing the contexts of the world.
This is a life-skill of the highest order. With it, a human being is
engaged with narrative, with the idea of life unfolding, and the
potential for change and variation. It is not difficult to suggest
that the sense of story allows emotional possibilities as well,
where the mind senses feelings in the presence of events, not just
as they happen in the moment, but as they happen in culmina-
tion of sequence and pattern. Further, involvement with a narrative allows us to see ourselves as potentially heroic in our own
lives, where we deserve to be our strongest selves.

The *second* way that cultural institutions help to construct the
learning of critical life skills is by offering a context for experi-
menting in the logics, processes, connections, and interrelations
of inquiry. Collections can offer immersion in a private framework for the pursuit of what one wants most to know. They al-

low the inquirer to express possibilities and create speculations while immersed in the presence of rich and visible evidence. The best museums and libraries offer paths for their pursuit beyond the institution.

Here the great gift of the cultural institution is tenuous and intangible. As learners come to recognize themselves engaged in the processes of thinking, asking questions, and making knowledge, they might well come to possess a literacy of self-designed inquiry for lifelong transformative learning. In this concept of literacy, the learner develops a skill at reading the unknowns latent in one life, and may, over time, come to understand how information leads one forward with a sense of control and power, in some cases toward a less dark, less stark, less accidental existence.

Accepting these roles for cultural institutions in the construction of literacies, we might strive to see our collections as settings for tool-based apprenticeships in the exploration and resolution of intellectual problems. How does historical (or scientific, or aesthetic) thinking work? What is the nature and meaning of handmade objects? How might a reader create a plan for systematic learning? How do human beings construct a social ecology? What is the role of knowledge in creating change? What is at risk, when we are thinking?

However much our lives may seem to unfold without design, there is in the mastery of tools and processes the abiding possibility of reducing our unknowns and the accidents that can shape us brutally. Clearly, in this world, those who understand tools and information will lead more informed, perhaps more designed lives; perhaps they are also likely to transmit the powers of an informed life to others as well. As we can understand in moments of national fear, sometimes the only thing we can control with confidence is what we know–if we can remain open to information and critically permeable to other voices.

The *third* quality of cultural institutions that seems an essential contribution to the construction of the individual life, is that libraries and museums, when they are fully open to the voices and interests of their users, are essential public spaces: forums for the expression and contemplation of other peoples' stories. As Hannah Arendt writes,

> Each time we talk about things that can be experienced only in privacy or intimacy, we bring them out into a sphere where they will assume a kind of reality that, their intensity notwithstanding, they never could have had before. . . . To live together in the world means essentially that a world of things is between those who have it in common, as a table is located between those who sit around it; the world, like every in-between, relates and separates [people] at the same time.[4]

Similarly, Maxine Greene writes of the idea that human beings need places where they can speak about their identities and understandings in public, and so confirm not only the similar existence of other people, but the reality of their own words and, in Greene's phrase, "lived experiences." The public space she describes is the community, that evanescent idea of a common world, held by all, and the subject of all the hopes and wishes that exist beyond the home and family. Greene writes powerfully about the rarity and power of the public space.

> There *is* no space where human beings, speaking and acting in their plurality, can appear before one another and realize the power they have simply in being together. And there surely is no such space in most of the schools. Nor is there the freedom experienced when young persons discover that they have the capacity to reach out and attain feelings, thoughts, and ways of being, hitherto unimagined—and even, perhaps, ways of acting on what they believe to be deficient, ways of transcending and going beyond.[5]

Greene cites examples of the courage required to create, in the name of community, a "common world." In another essay, she cites the anthropologist Clifford Geertz's suggestion that "the problem of integrating cultural life becomes one of 'making it possible for people inhabiting different worlds to have a genuine, and reciprocal, impact upon one another.'"[6]

Isn't this a reasonable description of the great problem that virtually every community culture faces? And might it not be a statement of mission for any cultural collection? And is this not what a great community means: a kind of collaborative, perpetually unfinished mind, always in search of dialogue not only about its future, and the meanings of its past, but also about the paths that each of us has made? Placing traditions of individualism aside, when we have such conversations in American collections, it is the community's way to pay attention to its continuous themes, its folkways, and its memories. We pay such attention in order to show, first, how deeply an interest in the life of the community is shared by all and, second, how the experience of creating this shared fabric has differed over time for individual citizens based on color, class, religion, language, and the steady interweaving of races and cultures.

To fulfill the concept of the community mind, it is important for a collection and its programs to capture many things. For any mindful, formative, thematic community conversation to happen, we need evidences of

- patterns of settlement, houses, and neighborhoods and all of the ways that "home" and "family" and "community" have meaning to us

- generational ways of passing the long-lasting knowledge of elders on to others

- dialogues that create a common table for generations to share

- governance, especially the politics of civic life, with its accompanying tensions over issues, and its need for informed participation and action

- economic life, comprising a balance of dying and emerging resources and technologies, interdependent services, information and know-how, industry in all its forms; the indicators of a productive community

- communication systems, and the community's patterns of isolation and connection, including the lines of language across communities

- formal and informal educational systems and their influence on the places a community values and creates for the transmission of knowledge

- institutions dedicated to religion, health, and public service and the ways they interpret their missions to the community

- the words and ways of the excluded, the sufferers, the activists, the seekers in our society

- what a community makes and treasures, how it embodies and interprets the meanings of experience in visual arts, performance, and the word

- unfinished, continuing, critical issues that require the attention of an entire community

- and, finally, evidences of how, in Clifford Geertz's words, "The culture of a people is an ensemble of texts."[7]

Collect these evidences and place them where they are visible and usable, and a community mind–a great, imaginative, communally owned artifact–is ready to be born.

From a farmer's perspective, Wendell Berry writes about how a community is a kind of knowledge, a form of mind:

> In its cultural aspect, the community is an order of memories preserved consciously in instructions, songs, and stories, and both consciously and unconsciously in *ways*. A healthy culture holds preserving knowledge *in place* for a *long* time. That is, the essential wisdom accumulates in the community much as fertility builds in the soil.[8][emphasis in original]

Every cultural institution *exists to give*. In contrast to elitist missions of the past, the contemporary cultural institution has been created and sustained by its community intentionally to give and regather itself again and again, to renew others and to replenish itself. In any cultural institution, in any community, however important the information given (the resources provided, the questions answered, the lectures delivered) it is never more important than the quality of generosity in the giving (the voices heard, the moments taken, the remembered question). The greatest value in our civic and democratic culture is not what its institutions keep, but what they give away, and how freely it is given.

Acts of giving are educative, communicative, community-building acts; apart from all other meanings, they express esteem. Exchange is complex. We must be present for each other if it is to happen. We must offer ourselves to others and receive others fairly. We may be unable to see the complexity of the transaction, because we are in it. We give it meaning in its moment, but its meaning is enhanced and changed by subsequent contexts and reflections, so its value is quickly unknown to us, even though we may be at its center.

As we know when we are in crisis, there are gifts that increase fluency and mastery over our most difficult moments of learning and becoming: calming systems of thought and observation in the presence of evidence, processes of reconstruction using voices and messages from the past, potential connections among separate evidences in a record, new ways of observing ourselves in process. These critical gifts transfer tools, language, and forms of thought to us, and allow us to remind ourselves of the future.

Cultural institutions allow us to experience an involvement with story, the creation of a narrative for sorting and constructing the multiple contexts of the world. In order to live lives not constructed by chaos or defined by the whims of others, we depend on the logics of narrative. The telling of a story—a community's story, say—not only captures an experience but also permits us to revisit it. The strongest cultural institution learns how to tell whole stories in the voices of its users. If the cultural institution is caringly constructed and given to its users, the story told is always moving, changing, and becoming, with the daring and clarity of a solo voice.

Great cultural institutions are institutions of mind as much as they are institutions of service. Their collections are informed by the implicit narratives of human contexts. They are dynamic. They think. They cause thinking. They absorb and reflect the thinking of others as though thought were a form of light. And the best cultural institutions are those most devoted to thinking *with* their publics—where thinking, as in the idea of the forum, is an inviting mutual event of language and feeling, self-presentation, and the incompleteness of mutual questioning.

Librarians, archivists, curators, and museum educators know that collections are not a static heritage, and that they comprise countless changing images and ideas; they require reinvention and rethinking, generation by generation. Perhaps we need to remind ourselves every day that we are not living or speaking a text that has already been written for us, but one that might best be described as flowing streams of the possible, generated in the moment-by-moment conversations and questions of users.

As an educator, I have found that it is increasingly important to think of our lives and works as improvisations grounded on the commodities of intelligence and self-respect. Every act of design or service undertaken by an institution is done in the name of its community of users and is a reflection of how the community of users is understood. Perhaps the gift of the great institution is the creation of collaborative users who come together to educate each other, appear before each other, and speak to each other in an effort at both mutual communication and the mutual illumination only authentic conversations create. Thinking of these possibilities, I remember once hearing Sam Miller, then the director of the Newark Museum (still admirably grounded in the mind of John Cotton Dana) refer to his institution as the "ceremonial center of the city." To me, this is a way of saying that the great cultural institution strives to give welcoming attention to the full fabric of its evolving world.

In my observations, the cultural institutions with the deepest integrity are those thinking most steadily about such gifts to the human culture nearby, the universe of learners at hand. I believe that our collections exist to bring learners together with the information and experiences that will resolve their critical incompletenesses. To do this, the mindful cultural institution needs to understand and participate fully in the worlds of citizens, including the lives of the least informed in the community, those with the smallest amount of power, the least access to tools, the most silent of citizens.

We all must know that without voices, people are more likely to lead lives shaped by accidents and discontinuities. And our work, or part of it, is to reduce the likelihood of purely accidental, partially understood existence. We must learn to think for the life of the community, to scan its horizons, and to act fearlessly for the lives of its learners. But understanding human voices and aspirations must always be cautious and respectful, and ought never to be an arrogant act. We know that every citizen, including the least in our family, may bear critical evidence for the future of the community mind.

Notes

1. Robert N. Bellah, et al., *The Good Society* (New York: Vintage, 1991), 5, 6.

2. Ivan Karp, "On Civil Society and Social Identity," in *Museums and Communities: The Politics of Public Culture*, ed. Ivan Karp, et al. (Washington, D.C.: Smithsonian Institution Press, 1992), 25.

3. Lauren Resnick, "Literacy in School and Out," *Daedalus* 119, no. 2 (1990): 169–185.

4. Hannah Arendt, *The Human Condition* (Chicago: University of Chicago Press, 1958), 50, 52.

5. Maxine Greene, "Public Education and the Public Space," *Educational Researcher* 11, no. 6 (June–July 1982): 4–9.

6. Clifford Geertz, *Local Knowledge* (New York: Basic Books, 1983), 161.

7. Clifford Geertz, *The Interpretation of Cultures* (New York: Basic Books, 1973), 452.

8. Wendell Berry, "People, Land, and Community," in *The Graywolf Annual Five: Multicultural Literacy*, ed. Rick Simonson and Scott Walker (St. Paul, Minn.: Graywolf Press, 1988), 50.

5

The Situation that Educates

I

It is not the educator, but the authentic situation for conversation created and sustained by the educator, that educates, by inviting the learner to go beyond the limits of previous knowledge. This authentic situation comprises more than skill, more than research, more than practice; it also comprises mystery, and an invitation to the unknown possibilities of inquiry. That is the best invitation to learn: to participate in a situation where questions are present, and in a process of inquiry that we may barely understand at its start. Join the conversation, the invitation implies, it is an authentic way to know something new and clearly your own.

Learning requires us all, teachers and learners, to construct and occupy a temporary architecture of risks and possibilities. No one acquires mastery without experiencing the risk of dwelling in the possible. Certainly it means lengthening the tether that binds a person to the familiar, trusted, and individually grounded past. This does not mean that a learner must leave behind the conventional, the routine, and the known. But it does mean that no one learns anything without walking to an edge of something and then moving beyond the edge—perhaps by falling over it accidentally.

Among the students I most admire, I observe that learning happens when they make an investment in their own risks and challenges, not mine. Learning for them has the best possibility of happening when choices are made, and when those choices cause patterns or processes of thought to change. The grounding questions of my classroom should always happen not in my voice but in the student's voice: What do I want to experience? What do I need to do next? What do I need to know next? What will engage me, and lead me forward?

No learners gain much from a task they already know how to do. Nor do they learn much from a question they have not freely asked themselves. As we know from the effects of television—an institution that induces passivity—distance and silence will also foster general disengagement and dysfunction; it is the opposite of the person becoming more specifically human. If all honest learning requires a situation of innovation and authorship, then the educator's task is to construct a place of trust, where risks can be taken, where work evolves from a passion to know, and where the best reward among participants is an increase in mutual regard.

It is important to me as an educator that the tasks I create for learners invite authentic risk and trust, lead them toward surprises, and are different from other experiences in their lives. My task is to assist what needs to happen, and I want to assure that it will happen in the right way. In the situations I design, I want people to learn how to move through knowledge structures confidently and to think critically about their passages. They will grasp and use their own language and imaginations as their primary tools, all other tools being secondary. They will experience the logics of process, its dead ends and revealed treasures. And their cognitive environments will change, become less temporary, and so will their senses of possible learning in the future. Over time, progress is made in their abilities to act usefully and independently in the presence of an unknown.

At least, this is what I want to have happen, and sometimes it does, but I am not quite certain how or why.

II

Museums and libraries are the critical institutions in American culture for people to renegotiate and expand the meanings of what they know and to consider ideas that are unfamiliar and often entirely new. People experience new information and connect it to what they understand from the past; they have conversations with companions and come to see new perspectives on their memories and education; they hear the voices and read the texts of scholars and curators. These are the ways the users of cultural institutions—as they stand among infinite combinations of objects, texts, and inquiries—come to grasp and experience the expansions and designs of mind made possible by a responsive situation where information appears.

These are physical spaces, but they are also active knowledge structures, always in motion and recombination. Cultural institutions are generative cognitive situations where the confluent qualities of objects, concepts, and juxtapositions compose a cognitive problem for their users. In any of these spaces, a person is challenged to construct an experience of meaning: to grasp inherent qualities and latent themes, and to understand their places along an exploratory path.

It is not enough to collect and provide, or simply to cause shallow awe and astonishment. The institution is responsible for creating a circumstance—a surrounding situation—where meanings are performed and intelligence is evoked in action. It is a circumstance that leads the user toward understanding through process. We grow through thoughts; we grow best through great, connected thoughts that come to us from insights. In the presence of a problem, the situation that educates helps us to perform the thoughts we need to perform in order to understand what we need to understand. When we leave that situation, we take understanding with us; when we return, it is with us still, ready for revival and renewal in the situation of its origin.

The responsive cultural institution expands the horizons of its users by constructing a situation for critical thinking, a place that offers no satisfying exit except through thought. The responsive setting encourages its users to pause and compare objects, texts, and processes; it makes information available under the control and design of the user; it inspires unplanned opportunities to discuss new images and information; it encourages its users to recognize and consider situations and ideas they have not considered before. This is an authentic challenge for an unfinished, continuously open life.

The situation that educates will assist a thoughtful user toward self-direction; it will expand awareness of data and sensation; it will permit the design of new knowledge through informed questions and logics; and (in Jerome Bruner's words) it will invite the learner to "go beyond the information given."[1] Cultural institutions, as transmitters of new knowledge and creators of informing situations, are the essential institutions for (again, in Bruner's words) "negotiating and renegotiating meaning and for explicating action"[2] in our culture. They epitomize places for what Robert Ennis says is the purpose of critical thinking: "deciding what to believe or do."[3]

Perhaps because museums and libraries can offer useful information at critical moments (or because, in their richness, they *induce* critical moments, moments of crisis when a potential turning point is present), museums and libraries appear to be watershed structures in our culture: after using them, certain things are not the same. Infusing new information into experience, cultural institutions work against entropy, restore balance or continuity, and allow a life to pause. In cultural institutions, knowledge structures offer taxonomies, histories, categories, vocabularies, insights—what we might call connective illuminations of knowledge. Among thoughtful people, observations, conversations, and other knowledge events cause thinking to open up, to admit possibilities, and to inspire cognitive change. When questions are asked, change begins.

In an essay advocating an "emancipatory" theory of communication, Klaus Krippendorff defines constrained situations as traps, or "closed systems of reality constructions, institutionalized attitudes, rationalizations, beliefs, habits of thought and actions." In such settings, the horizon of possibility we can imagine is better characterized by constraints than by expansions. "A closed system offers the beholder coherent explanations, selectively admits experiences consistent with it, and suppresses feelings that do not fit. In a closed system all acts of observation, judgment, elaboration, all cognitions are dedicated to the maintenance . . . of the system's identity."[4] When we enter a closed cultural institution of this kind, we enter on its terms only—not our own—and throughout our experience there, we are given scant opportunity to assert our own questions or preferences as users.

In contrast, a situation that educates is an open system, invested in creating a place for unpredicted, inventive thoughts. It may offer contradictions, controversies, and alternative perspectives in order to suggest that a person can design knowledge independently and privately. It may be a situation that fearlessly invites unanswerable questions and allows them to fill our thoughts.

III

In these open situations, a guiding concept is most important: The museum user is an asker of questions and a user of information. This user is capable of making sense personally with appropriate data and tools in hand. Part of the institution's contract with the user is to provide useful information or to provide a way to find it.

Brenda Dervin has written about the need to see a user as a "person at a particular moment in time and space, rather than across time and space."[5] The person lives now, in a situation now, with immediate complexities and constraints. The person experiences gaps in making sense of the world and so must ask questions. The person is capable of defining goals within an information system and so must understand its limits. The person has strategies for using information, like browsing, grouping, interpreting; and the person can apply dimensions astutely to knowledge, categorizing it according to timeliness, relevance, depth, and apparent accuracy. Data, sensation, design, logic—all invite critical thinking and planning; all lead to the insights that reorganize knowledge.

A situation that recognizes its users in this way shows an implicit respect, an understanding that the person has a history and a future as a learner, and that there is the likelihood of continuous self-informing experiences to follow. The institution recognizes, as well, that its value is proven only in what follows its use. If the library or museum does not reach into the world where its users live, go to work, speak to others, enact partnerships, and reflect on the larger issues of one life, it has not gone beyond itself.

I believe that people are led to museums and libraries by hope, expectation, and need, and by the possibility of discovering change through their thoughts and experiences. Cultural institutions are able to meet and stimulate these hopes, expectations, and needs, and further, to evoke in their users intense hungers for knowledge, insight, and understanding. Information and assistance freely given are forms of nourishment for these hungers. When the situation that educates is extended beyond the institution, it is evidence that such hungers, even when nourished, do not go away but can be sustained with great satisfaction over the lifespan.

In my earliest research, I observed that, in libraries, *the information given is never more important than the quality of the giving.*[6] Among the qualities of the giving are these:

- The information given should fit the user.
- The information given should assist in developing language.
- The information given should involve the collaboration and assent of the user. Partnership or apprenticeship is also implied.
- The information given should respond to a question asked by the user.
- The information given should end with a question and lead to another question.

Informed conversations, in situations where more than one voice can be heard, where newly named ideas can be spoken and tried out, and where the productive interdependencies of persons and institutions can be explored, constitute what Krippendorff calls "emancipatory discourse." In this way, situations that educate in cultural institutions are necessary in democratic cultures. They fulfill a promise to see the person as an independent agent, respect the person as an autonomous actor, and assist the person in forward motion, toward a learning life.

IV

I have suggested to my students that, during visits to museums, they keep track of their experiences on two levels. Primarily, I want them to document what they see, observe, and take in; these are the evidences of the museum experience, the educative qualities that induce reflection and judgment. But I also ask them to keep track of occasional moments when they feel confused, or when something flashes with insight, or when an exhibition or a moment makes sudden, perfect sense. These are the moments of personal or emotional resonance, and the experience is part of a private interior passage. One way to grasp and hold these observations is by using a tape recorder, speaking into it as the flow of events moves the user from the moment of entrance until departure. The tape recording becomes a direct evidence of the sequences of events and perceptions, field based, unrevised, and uninterpreted. (Incidentally, such tapes remind the listener of the easily neglected aural qualities of museum experiences and other ambient phenomena difficult to capture in written field notes.)

A student once casually shared with me a recording of her visit to the American Museum of Natural History. She documented her arrival, her rush to a Naturemax film, observations on the Northwest Coast objects, and then the mollusks, the artifacts of the Maya, and, after a few hours, the minerals and gems. As I listened, I had a clear image of where she was in the museum at every step and what she was seeing. As I heard her voice, I realized that I could enter this museum as though it were the house of my childhood, walk down its corridors, make a turn or two and look, say, directly at the mountain lion or the American bison, immobile in their dioramas, and then beyond, into the painted distance on the wall—all while sitting at my desk. Listening to that tape—and to other recordings I have made of my own observations—I found that the museum was not simply a memory of intellectual encounters, but a whole, specific, intact space for me, and, to the moment of this writing, it is known to me as an environment with its own powerful reality.

We keep such spaces in mind as though they were rooms in the memory palaces of the past.[7] In the epistemic, or knowledge generating, setting, the quality of place communicates order, structure, and process. Describing the epistemic institution, Chapin and Klein write, "The architectural divisions and spatial organizations of museums create metaphors for the divisions of the house of knowledge."[8] (These divisions create more than metaphors, I will add. For example, at the American Museum of Natural History, users walk among dinosaurs following a cladistic tree embedded in the floor tiles, experiencing a passage among not only fossilized remains, but also among phylogenetic relationships.)

Enter any thoughtfully constructed museum or library and you have entered a design for mindful use, and perhaps the physical embodiment of a mind itself, a cognitive environment—a space that captures a way of thinking. Cultural institutions might be considered to be laboratories for the exploration of the continuities among objects and ideas. The metaphor also implies the ambient energies of inquiry, nearly palpable in the intense devotions of thoughtful users. Although they rarely offer clear paths for the exploration of their contents, museums and libraries occur in the lives of users spatially; mastery of a cultural institution as a user often implies simply holding its rooms in mind.

To refer to cultural institutions as cognitive *laboratories* is to imply functions and behaviors associated with measurement, control, notation, and discovery. To allude to *energies* in museums and libraries is to imply a process, or a kind of flow. When I look for *clear paths* or allude to *perspectives*, or *continuities*, and when I refer to the value of *design* in our experiences, I am offering spatial ideas. My implication is that our understanding and use of a cultural institution, particularly a museum, is spatial; the situation that educates is a physical place we enter, and what we do in it, even against the odds, is find our way, generating knowledge as we go.

V

The educative structure of any institution can be mapped, first as a physical environment, and second as more than a physical environment. It is possible for one map to capture both the physical and conceptual spaces of a cultural institution, but it is rare to find that an institution has done this. The standard physical map addresses the fundamental problem for every user: finding the physical way toward someplace in the setting, to have an experience that will make a difference in thought or memory, despite the constraints of time. Using the words of cognitive researchers, a cultural institution can be seen as an example of a "complex problem space,"[9] a challenging but navigable environment with internal logics, routes of access to specific objectives, and supportive information systems designed to advance the cognitive skills most valued in the setting.

The physical map of a collection can offer a sense of location and direction, allowing a self-directing user to plan, to think of a future step, and to manage the challenges of the immediate physical environment. A cultural institution can also be mapped usefully as a system of concepts or defining ideas. The nature of the institutional mission and its user community might suggest initial guidance for such maps. Just as the physical map allows the user to move forward deliberately, the mapping or indexing of concepts and themes allows narrative and textual qualities to anchor the user's exploration in ideas, and it deepens the resonance of the physical space as well. Simple quotations from naturalists, scientists, philosophers, artists, or even the words of wise museum users can remind us of the ideas and structures at hand.

Conceptual mapping helps to make cognitive connections possible, while creating loosely ordered frames for thinking. These frames enhance not only the user's senses of design, structure and logic, they also create situations that make it likely for thoughts to change. As any thoughtful librarian knows, one value of a conceptual structure is that it impels the progress of dedicated exploratory thought. Another value of structure for our cognitive process is the progressive frame it provides for encountering an unknown—our expectation of order allows us to recognize the exquisite surprise when it steps out of line or off the shelf to awaken us.

To return to a particular space, twenty years ago, when I was beginning to think systematically about cultural institutions, the most important lessons I constructed for myself occurred at the American Museum of Natural History in New York City. The director of education, Malcolm Arth, allowed me generous hours there with him and with his colleagues, in order to figure out for myself what that great place was about, what it does, and what it means for learners. One of the ways I documented my observations was by carrying out what I called "concept inventories," focusing on particular rooms in the museum, listing objects and specimens, nomenclature, label texts, illustrations, physical models—and all of the sensory data I could perceive as a sensing organism in the setting.

I projected potential contexts for decontextualized evidence. I sought to understand the place of every object I could see in my emerging sense of the classification system. I attempted to imagine discoveries and empirical research that confirmed them. I also developed broad frameworks in my notebooks, consisting of the knowledge presented: concepts and generalizations having to do (as I thought) with the weights and values of the ideas presented, and a developing notion of "conceptual density," my term for an overabundance of stimuli in museums.

My inventory process was dense indeed, and exhausting. For example, my notes about Neanderthals, taken in the Hall of Man in Asia, include concepts like "Domestication," "Social groups," "Value of fire," "Effects of tools," "Ritual," "Cognition," and "Afterlife." These terms, derived from the objects and texts at hand, served as organizers for my observations and suppositions. Over time and consistent observations, a narrative, a story of the invisible parts of Neanderthal "experience" came into my words. Perhaps more important, an understanding of these concepts *needed to emerge* before I was able to understand and grasp in my own way the value and meaning of the objects presented. I imagined what it might have meant (in my own primitive mind) to live a Neanderthal life, see a Neanderthal landscape and horizon, and to shape my life with a Neanderthal hand.

In other informing settings, and other situations that educate, such structures as concept maps[10] make the institution more powerful as an instrument of knowledge; they suggest possible frames for thought and experience and serve as guiding cognitive ideas that allow a user to design and redesign learning. In a library, where structure is overtly systematic and pervasive to all experiences of discovery, such concept maps may already exist, latent in indices, thesauri, and taxonomies. Generic concept maps—documents that encourage critical thoughts, comparisons, and the logics of discovery—can also be developed using heuristic questions or critical concepts derived from scholarly processes. In specific situations, the variable and contrary notions of individual scholars may be apposite ways to model or provoke new thinking.

Every museum or library map is a tentative and general tool, offering exploratory ways to think through inevitable densities. There is, of course, good thinking to be done when we become lost: Where am I? Where am I going? What do I want to happen next?

VI

Jean Lave and Etienne Wenger make it clear that an educative situation is created to make deeper engagements with the world more possible. Education does not happen in the abstract, apart from a world of continuities and connections. "Learning," they write, "is an integral part of generative social practice in the lived-in world."[11] In such situations, "Learning, thinking, and knowing are relations among people in activity in, with, and arising from the socially and culturally structured world."[12]

Brown, Collins, and Duguid describe a fundamental idea of situated cognition.

> People who use tools actively rather than just acquire them . . . build an increasingly rich implicit understanding of the world in which they use the tools and of the tools themselves. . . . Learning how to use a tool involves far more than can be accounted for in any set of explicit rules. The occasions for use arise directly out of the context of activities of each community that uses the tool, framed by the way members of that community see the world. . . . To learn to use tools as practitioners use them, a student, like an apprentice, must enter that community and its culture.[13]

The activities that learners must complete to make sense of complex institutional situations should not be limited to organized classes and tours, but should reflect what Lave and Wenger call "the organization of the community of practice."[14] In a cultural institution, for example, what should be transmitted is the knowledge held in place by its community of users. We learn about fishing through an engagement with the lives of fishers; we come to understand a tapestry as we intuitively follow the weaver's handwork; we grasp the process of connecting ideas by observing such connections in the lives of others.

Consequently, for the users of museums and libraries, conceptual groundings are best presented to learners through contextually situated experiences, in the presence of artifacts and information in situations of use; that is, where authentic (coherent, grounded, purposeful) activities and discourses flow. Support is best given by well-informed human agents—librarians, educators, curators, and expert explainers—who are attentive to process. In every cultural institution, the events of process and the situations of encounter warrant attention.

Given the words, observations, and guidance of informed others, the learner in the situation is enabled to conduct a temporary immersion in the pursuit of something new and promising. Though its content may be evanescent and even improvisational, the situation for learning is a physical situation, a place where people go to seek information and knowledge, to interpret alone or with others, and to find guidance through human relationships. They think actively, explore possibilities, and expand experiences in order to become different persons. This is learning in an adult life.

When the focus of a cultural institution is moved from didacticism toward a contextually situated knowledge structure, its users can become participants in the continuities, values, and meanings of the living, constructive environment. For example, an institution's system of activities for learning any topic might involve opportunities to see examples and to understand contexts; it might provide visible opportunities to understand the history of a collection, its development and preservation. An institution's contributions to community development and its engagements with the living culture nearby are evidences of the museum itself in context.

Whenever we see such elements as community volunteers and docents; open storage, open laboratory, and construction areas; information about missions, processes, changes, and governance; and explainers and guides of all ages, we are seeing visible structures that draw users into the cultural institution as participants. If we can come to see each museum and library as a community of practice—"a set of relations among persons, activity, and world, over time and in relation with other . . . communities of practice"[15]—then we might begin to see the user as a person on an extended journey, moving and thinking, carried among situations for learning by a community's systemic cognitive flow.

What the learner can come to know along this way is not anything to be taught outright or prescribed by a curriculum. Rather, in practice, "knowing is inherent in the growth and transformations of identities" and is situated within the relatively unpredictable structure and substance of activities, "relations among practitioners, their practice, [and] the artifacts of that practice."[16] The learner in the situation is given an opportunity to witness the construction and presentation of knowledge, and perhaps even to assist as an apprentice in this construction. At its most effective, the situation for cognition allows the learner to be intensely present in a complex world of thought and action.

Along this way, a museum or library can become a place where people come to experience brief immersions in the values and culture of the institution, as they are embodied in the practice community of the setting. An awareness of the intellectually active institution can be a form of cognitive apprenticeship. For the apprentice, as Lave and Wenger write, "learning is itself an improvised practice: A learning curriculum unfolds in opportunities for engagements in practice. It is not specified as a set of dictates."[17]

VII

The primary themes in this essay originate with a presentation prepared for a conference of the New York City Museum Educators Roundtable at the American Museum of Natural History, called "Museums and a Sense of Place." When that theme was announced, I thought I had little to contribute, until I looked closely at the language of the cognitive psychologists whose writings litter my desk.

When speaking of cognition, for example, Lave and Wenger use the word "situation" as a way to describe a place where the mind's engagement can thrive. The most prominent of spatial metaphors is Lev Vygotsky's idea of the "zone of proximal development," the realm where we try out our tentative knowledge in the beckoning presence of a more capable peer, a nurturing person who, by offering assistance and invitation, helps us to move forward from what we know now, toward new levels of skill and understanding. The forward motion of development in this zone is propelled by the more capable other, who, by suggesting and evoking our own abilities and desired skills, invites us to develop them. It is a concept that deserves application to all human transformation. The ideas of the proximal zone and its companion, apprenticeship, are at the core of cognitive activity in cultural institutions.

My interest lies in the idea that the entire cultural institution, even without the identifiable proximal helper, is a zone of proximal development, a critical zone, constructed in such a way that we are always inclining forward, toward a new level of insight, understanding, or experience. In a well-constructed setting, we are always on the edge of seeing something before us or within us that moves us beyond our initial state of mind. I believe that cognizant human beings are always pushing toward the verge of insight and will engage in forward motion if useful and attractive problems and situations for learning are presented to them. Learners learn in promising situations, where the possibilities of response are robust and constructive.

For example, Brown and Reeve have reported that, when working alone, children tend to create personal structures to serve as their own developmental scaffolds—they call them "zones of competence," in comparison to Vygotsky's "zones of proximal development."[18]

> Children learn in situations where there is no obvious guidance, no feedback other than their own satisfaction, and no external pressure to improve or change. In a very real sense they act as little scientists, creating [theories] that they challenge, extend, and modify on their own. The child is not only a problem solver but also a problem creator—a metaphor that has much in keeping with scientific thinking.[19]

Eleanor Duckworth also describes situations where children can raise the right questions for themselves and move themselves forward without adult intervention.

> The right question at the right time can move children to peaks in their thinking that result in significant steps forward and real intellectual excitement; . . . although it is almost impossible for an adult to know exactly the right time to ask a specific question of a specific child . . . children can raise the right question for themselves if the setting is right.

"Once the right question is raised," she continues, "they are moved to tax themselves to the fullest to find an answer."[20]

I think that these observations are not limited to children as learners; I think they are true of all learners. In situations where the possibilities of independent learning are made clear, an opportunity to encounter powerful objects or ideas without the mediation of an instructor would lead any learner naturally on, toward insight and competence. Consequently, for children and adults in cultural institutions, it is important to conceive and create situations where learners are encouraged and enabled to advance their own becoming by thinking more and more like themselves, free to accept or modify the more orthodox and less immediate perspectives of curators, educators, critics, and historians.[21] It is the task of all learners, literally, to make up their own minds, among other minds.

Learners in museums deserve to experience and appreciate the qualities of cognitive companionship and cognitive apprenticeship frequently denied in the denser situations of school. Citing an array of researchers, Sylvia Farnham-Diggory describes four principles of an apprenticeship model for education, based on the idea of direct learning of skills, as it typically occurs in workplace apprenticeships.[22] The workplace she describes is the "workplace of the mind," however, and these are some of the ways we need to understand it.

1. Human minds are designed for complex, situated learning. . . . Human brains are constructed to deal with richly complex environments, to make sense out of their experiences, and to store knowledge that is useful in coping with new ones. . . . We can and do make sense out of a swirl of events. We can and do learn to identify important goals, cues, and strategies.

2. Expert models must participate in the instructional program. Human expertise is complicated. It cannot be obtained by adding up a list of facts to be acquired, skills to be demonstrated, and problems to be solved. Much expert knowledge is tacit: it cannot be articulated. But it can be transmitted. By working with an expert gardener you can

become one yourself. The presence of experts in a learning situation is the only way to ensure that instructional objectives are fully represented.

3. Education must begin where the student is. . . . It isn't enough to march the student through a series of preplanned lessons, grading her as she goes along. . . . Minds are not empty vessels that parents and teachers fill up. . . . All students entering a new domain of knowledge are, in fact, junior versions of experts. They have some of the frameworks. They have the rudiments of every type of knowledge that experts have. This is why cognitive and developmental science emphasizes the importance of basing instruction on what a beginner brings to a learning situation.

4. Human learning is a social enterprise. . . . Intelligence, in this model, instead of being held to reside in the individual, is held to reside in the group. Working together, the group can produce a brilliant collective product that no individual could have been expected to produce alone. Human learning, the accumulation of the knowledge that has produced modern civilization, is a social enterprise. It has never been the case in real life that rows of individuals, sitting behind desks, have each been charged with solving the same problem to the same level of competence.[23]

The cultural institution offers itself to learners as a rare experience for discovering, mining, and owning one's own thoughts, taking charge of and mastering the process of one's own becoming. We need to know the best ways for assisting people to make choices, to choose to participate fully in the design of their own experiences and lives, and to discover the potential power of a specific, watershed experience to change all other experiences. What can the museum do to provoke a person to cross an edge in thought, to become so deeply engaged that not only the experience, but also the thinking surrounding it becomes part of the watershed moment?

Howard Gardner, in *The Unschooled Mind*, finds the museum's potential as a situation for apprenticeship to be a powerful model.

In such long-term relationships, novices have the opportunity to witness on a daily basis the reasons for various skills, procedures, concepts, and symbolic and notational systems. They observe competent adults moving readily and naturally from one external or internal way of representing knowledge to another. They experience firsthand the consequences of a misguided or misconceived analysis, even as they gain pleasure when a well-thought-out procedure works properly. They undergo a transition from a situation in which much of what they do is based on adult models to one in which they are trying out their own approaches, perhaps with some support or criticism from the master. They can discuss alternatives with more accomplished peers, just as they can provide assistance to peers who have recently joined the team. All these options, it seems to me, guide the student toward that state of enablement—exhibiting the capacity to use skills and concepts in an appropriate way—that is the hallmark of emerging understanding.[24]

There is another quality of emergence that Gardner does not acknowledge: the transformation of the learner's emerging sense of self as an aware and competent individual, one becoming capable of holding, representing, and leading in the communication of knowledge that might be inspiring to others. These characteristics bring Csikszentmihalyi's concept of "optimal flow" to mind, as it might be experienced in the museum: the centering of attention on a specific activity, the exclusion of extraneous influences, loss of personal importance and self-consciousness, incremental skill development in order to overcome challenges, and clear goals and feedback from the environment, leading to intrinsic satisfaction.[25]

VIII

When I am in museums without companions, I have often found my experiences exalting, but I have also found them encapsulating and disconnective, because I am alone. The situation of the lone user is somewhat challenging: In the presence of brilliant ideas, extraordinary objects, and knowledge without end, having great new thoughts to try out and test, I have no one to turn or talk to.

Sometimes I am not sure that I really want to turn to someone else, but it seems to me that I feel so isolated and voiceless because there is no place in the situation where people can present themselves and their ideas *of* the museum, *in* the museum. In recent years, innocuous comment books and occasionally more innovative forms of documenting user experiences (focus groups, videotaped interviews) have appeared. But until, then billions of users have moved through cultural institutions without once having the opportunity to utter a word or convey a thought that might have mattered critically to the institution itself. What kinds of cultural institutions might we have now, had someone cared to ask and listen thirty years ago? What would we know today if we had redefined our libraries and museums as places where users are invited to express their experiences as well as to receive the knowledge they seek?

I advocate that educative cultural institutions should assure their users of private, individual experiences; but it is also my advocacy that there is great value in creating situations for dialogue and exchange with other learners. Collaborative engagements—where the user and the institution acknowledge their mutual interests and interdependencies—might involve the framing of an intellectual problem in the setting, or it might comprise explorations of strategies, perhaps including investigations in other institutions. In dialogues between user and user, ideas can be tested and advice can be given. The presence of an educative agent—the best model for this person is the reference librarian—helps the user to reframe the problem within the contexts of the collections offered. When the cultural institution enters a collaboration with its users, it not only can hear eyewitness accounts of experience and hope; it can also find its own public voice as an educative situation.

We can assume that generative situations where collaboration is fostered are good for thinking and working. For example, Barbara Rogoff reports a 1937 study on "productive collaboration" involving problem solving with artworks. Children who collaborated in the discussions and activities of the experiment showed increases in mental activities and concentration. They worked more systematically than noncollaborators. When the attention of one partner flagged, it was revived by another.[26] (My adult students report that they have far more useful, even more illuminating experiences when they are present in institutions with informed, observant companions.)

In the 1937 experiment, collaborating children also showed improvements in some of the qualities that Jerome Bruner related to intuition: the will to take an initial step, an open attitude toward work and risk taking, and greater ease in applying and receiving critical judgments.[27] "In collaboration," Rogoff writes in *Apprenticeship in Thinking*, "the partners engage in a critical process in which the achievement of intersubjectivity [shared awareness based on a common focus of attention] leads to new solutions."[28] In collaborations, the use of a shared language permits naming, connecting, and categorizing objects, the negotiation of hypotheses, and over all, a mutually structured understanding of processes and events. The development of language contributes to intersubjectivity in exploratory work, acting as a system for bridging and transmitting the differences between "one understanding of a situation and another."[29]

Authentic thought and response, or instinctive understanding of the kind that we rarely experience in our schooling—the giving of oneself over, intellect and emotion, to the unfinished processes of knowing something—can occur only in a situation where such activities are actively occurring in more lives than one, where learners are invited to join in these practices, and where a culture of expert practice is continuously developing.

To envision and re-create cultural institutions as public, collaborative communities is especially challenging when the situation, in the words of Collins, Brown, and Newman, is a "cognitive domain where many of the relevant processes and inferences are tacit and hidden."[30] The restoration of a public, educative culture will require the voices of champions, able to advance learner-centered policies, and articulate aloud the value of exploring an institution and its instrumental power.

IX

Cognition is grounded in social relationships and processes, and advanced by participation. Studying the clustered households of a Hispanic community in Arizona, Moll and Greenberg[31] found extensive and proliferating systems for sharing and exchanging funds of knowledge—networks of household-centered collectives holding essential information, strategic skills and operations, human and material resources—transmitted by identifiable pedagogies and socially organized learning. "It is unnecessary and unfeasible for individual persons or households to possess all this knowledge; when needed, such knowledge is available and accessible through social networks."[32] When the household—surely a situation that educates—is seen as a system of knowledge, it is evident that the transmission of information and practice does not occur in abstract ways, but in response to authentic questions and needs to know. These social relations provide a motive and a context for acquiring and applying knowledge. In such contexts, "Funds of knowledge are manifested through events or activities"; they are not possessions or traits of people in the family but characteristics of people-in-an-activity.[33]

These shared systems of support for the cognitive survival of individuals are enduring, reciprocal, and based on trust. They assist learning by creating extensive zones for the possible, where inexperienced performers are assisted and knowledge is mediated by elders or (in Vygotsky's words) more capable peers. Though it may be tenuous to transplant these observations into the different contexts of cultural institutions, among multiple generations and forms of knowledge, it is useful to suggest that vast, diverse, relevant funds of knowledge are present in users as well as in educators, curators, and librarians.

We are challenged to find ways to invite the hidden-yet-relevant funds of knowledge and strategic problem solving to emerge, to give them voices, and to make them fully present in a situation that educates. In closed, rigid, and constrained environments, these funds may be forever silent and unavailable to learners engaged in the construction of knowledge.

But in educative institutions where diverse funds of private knowledge can find public voices, our critical resources for knowledge are expanded. The experience and memory of the user, the deeper critical mastery of the librarian or curator, the communicative and nurturing stance of the educator could become interactive, evocative resources. These might enable not only the participation and cognitive survival of the learner in a tentative world, but also the transformation of the insular cultural institution into an open community of conversation and practice.

We encounter the situation that educates as a place where human beings speak their thoughts, where they are encouraged to complete the presence of memories, objects, concepts, dreams, and possibilities. Objects and knowledge have no meaning without a person standing in their presence, ready to speak and listen. Always our task remains to go beyond where we are, without hesitation or fear, toward new encounters with the distant, the incomplete, and the unknown, our fearless energy for knowledge grounded in our words and the institutional structures that illuminate our journey through them.

Notes

This essay is based on presentations at gatherings of the New York City Museum Educators Roundtable, the Task Force on the Future of Children at the Children's Museum of Indianapolis, and the Association of Youth Museums.

1. Jerome Bruner, "Going beyond the Information Given," in *Beyond the Information Given: Studies in the Psychology of Knowing*, ed. J. M. Anglin (New York: W. W. Norton, 1973), 218–238.

2. Jerome Bruner, *Actual Minds, Possible Worlds* (Cambridge, Mass.: Harvard University Press, 1986).

3. Robert Ennis, "A Taxonomy of Critical Thinking Dispositions and Abilities," in *Teaching Thinking Skills: Theory and Practice*, ed. J. B. Baron and R. J. Sternberg (New York: W. H. Freeman, 1987), 9–26.

4. Klaus Krippendorff, "The Power of Communication and the Communication of Power: Toward an Emancipatory Theory of Communication," *Communication* 12 (1989): 175–196.

5. Brenda Dervin, "Users as Research Inventions: How Research Categories Perpetuate Inequities," *Journal of Communication* 39, no. 3 (1989): 216–232.

6. David Carr, "The Agent and the Learner: Interactions in Assisted Adult Library Learning," *Public Library Quarterly* 2, no. 2 (Summer 1980): 3–19.

7. See, for example: Frances A. Yates, *The Art of Memory* (Chicago: University of Chicago Press, 1966); Jonathan D. Spence, *The Memory Palace of Matteo Ricci* (New York: Viking Penguin, 1984).

8. D. Chapin and S. Klein, "The Epistemic Museum," *Museum News* 71, no. 4 (July/August 1992): 61.

9. Cognition and Technology Group at Vanderbilt, "Anchored Instruction and Its Relationship to Situated Cognition," *Educational Researcher* 19, no. 6 (1990): 3–10.

10. See Joseph D. Novak and D. Bob Gowin, *Learning How to Learn* (New York: Cambridge University Press, 1984).

11. Jean Lave and Etienne Wenger, *Situated Learning: Legitimate Peripheral Participation* (New York: Cambridge University Press, 1991), 35.

12. Lave and Wenger, *Situated Learning*, 51.

13. John Seely Brown, A. Collins, and P. Duguid, "Situated Cognition and the Culture of Learning," *Educational Researcher* 18, no. 1 (1989): 33.

14. Lave and Wenger, *Situated Learning*, 94.

15. Lave and Wenger, *Situated Learning*, 98.

16. Lave and Wenger, *Situated Learning*, 122.

17. Lave and Wenger, *Situated Learning*, 93.

18. A. L. Brown and R. A. Reeve, "Bandwidths of Competence: The Role of Supportive Contests in Learning and Development," in *Development and Learning: Conflict or Congruence,* ed. L. S. Liben (Hillsdale, N.J.: Lawrence Erlbaum, 1987), 171–223.

19. Brown and Reeve, "Bandwidths of Competence," 199.

20. Eleanor Duckworth, *"The Having of Wonderful Ideas" and Other Essays on Teaching and Learning* (New York: Teachers College Press, 1987), 5.

21. I want to make clear that I believe expertise to be valuable. At the right moment, the incisive expert's provocative thought can move a learner along toward insight. Three exemplary exhibitions where

such provocations occur have been superbly documented by these volumes:

Joseph Kosuth, *The Play of the Unmentionable* (New York: The New Press, 1992).

Arthur Danto et al., *Art/Artifact: African Art in Anthropology Collections* (New York: Center for African Art, 1988).

Fred Wilson, *Mining the Museum: An Installation* (Baltimore: Contemporary, 1994).

In these exhibitions, tensions between objects and texts led users inexorably to explore their own assumptions and values, and so to see for themselves the possibilities of their own crafted truths. [For thinking on the art museum as a setting for active dialogues, see also Kynaston McShine, *The Museum as Muse: Artists Reflect* (New York: Museum of Modern Art, 1999); James Putnam, *Art and Artifact: The Museum as Medium* (New York: Thames and Hudson, 2001); and *The Discursive Museum*, ed. Peter Noever (Vienna: MAK, 2001.)]

22. Sylvia Farnham-Diggory, *Schooling* (Cambridge, Mass.: Harvard University Press, 1990).

23. Farnham-Diggory, *Schooling*, 56–66.

24. Howard Gardner, *The Unschooled Mind* (New York: Basic Books, 1991), 202–203.

25. Adapted from Mihalyi Csikszentmihalyi and Rick E. Robinson, *The Art of Seeing: An Interpretation of the Aesthetic Encounter* (Malibu, Calif.: J. P. Getty Museum, 1990), 8.

26. Barbara Rogoff, *Apprenticeship in Thinking* (New York: Oxford University Press, 1990), 180–183.

27. Jerome S. Bruner, *The Relevance of Education*, ed. Anita Gil (New York: W. W. Norton, 1971), 82–97.

28. Rogoff, *Apprenticeship in Thinking*, 183.

29. Rogoff, *Apprenticeship in Thinking*, 71.

30. A. Collins, J. S. Brown, and S. E. Newman, "Cognitive Apprenticeship: Teaching the Crafts of Reading, Writing and Mathematics," in *Knowing, Learning and Instruction: Essays in Honor of Robert Glaser*, ed. L. Resnick (Hillsdale, N.J.: Lawrence Erlbaum, 1989), 488.

31. L. C. Moll and J. B. Greenberg, "Creating Zones of Possibilities: Combining Social Contexts for Instruction," in *Vygotsky and Education*, ed. L. C. Moll (New York: Cambridge University Press, 1990), 319–348.

32. Moll and Greenberg, "Creating Zones of Possibilities," 323.

33. Moll and Greenberg, "Creating Zones of Possibilities," 326.

6

A Poetics of Questions

What is it? What holds the thing in our minds—the basket, the bowl, the Fabergé egg, the moons of Jupiter, Australopithecine bones, our view of events along the Little Big Horn River? What keeps it vivid in our imaginative reach and grasp? How was it to have lived then and to have seen this? (It must have been so.) How did this object, this event, happen? (It must have been this way.) What could it have meant to witness this? (It would have meant this. It could have meant that.) What do I need to know next?

I

A human being *becoming* is the critical center of the entire cultural institution—*critical*, because museums and libraries exist to assist changes, passages, and transformations; *critical*, because experiences in history, art, or analysis can induce a turning point in the knowledge that grounds us; and *critical*, because the fate of our question leads us toward differences in how and what we learn.

A question implies motion. As individuals in the process of becoming, our integrity is shaped over time by the quality of the questions we ask and sustain, and how they move us along. It is our good questions, far more than any answer we may settle on, that urge us forward cognitively. If a question implies motion, think of each inquiry we build as a little engine of cognition. We use our intellectual strength to keep it on its track and get us to a new station.

A life is shaped by its formative institutions and its continuing, unfinished issues. Our passage of personal change or transformation is just as crafted as an artifact or a discovery emerging from our encounters with the unknown. It has the same roughnesses and tentative forms. It seems permanently unfinished. The good question places the past at risk. It introduces disorder and challenge. It marks our progress toward change. It can stay with us over our lifespan and become our own question for life. When we step into the museum or the library we have willed ourselves to experience the possibilities of change, sometimes great change, driven by our unfinished issues.

We undertake a lifelong, continuous process that is both *toward* integrity and *of* integrity. Except for death, there is no end to the possibilities of purpose and coherence in one life. Our best questions construct the best of those possibilities.

I believe that the center of an educator's definitive purpose, no matter what the institution, is to construct a situation where questions can find form. This is also the purpose of using cultural institutions, seeing exhibitions, and seeking ideas through information. Even the sacred repository invites wonder. Any institution ought to express the unknown as well as the known, and issue invitations for the user to explore each, with tools at hand and voices in mind.[1] To focus the evolving mind on the unknown is the most useful, most educative gift.

The conduct of inquiry in cultural institutions is a profound value; the responsibility of cultural institutions in this process of becoming through questions cannot be overstated. In the public world we inhabit, there is no comparable place—authoritative, venerable, reflective—for a thoughtful person to take a good question and work on it. And there is nowhere else where the inspiring traces of other questioning human beings are so clearly present.

II

In libraries, museums, and other cultural institutions, we most need to understand the resonances, complexities, and possibilities of the user's leading questions. We need to understand, in our lives and those of others, the tendrils that connect what we ask now to what has been asked by others before us, and sought before, and perhaps answered before. By the resonant question, we move forward, across the edges of the everyday, and over the bridges our lives are meant to be. As educators, we need to learn how to invite and shape in other minds the emergent and sometimes silent question. As we look at ourselves and other learners, we know that critical, perhaps unanswerable questioning is central to tacit processes of becoming in a learning life.

Here are three poems by Pablo Neruda, from his final work, *The Book of Questions.*[2]

> IX
> Is the sun the same as yesterday's
> or is this fire different from that fire?
> How do we thank the clouds
> for their fleeting abundance?
> From where does the thundercloud come
> with its black sacks of tears?
> Where are all those names
> sweet as the cakes of yesteryear?
> Where did they go, the Donaldas,
> the Clorindas, the Eduvigises?

> XLIV
> Where is the child I was,
> still inside me or gone?
> Does he know that I never loved him
> and that he never loved me?

Why did we spend so much time
growing up only to separate?
Why did we both not die
when my childhood died?
And why does my skeleton pursue me
if my soul has fallen away?

XLIII
Who was she who made love to you
in your dream, while you slept?
Where do the things in dreams go?
Do they pass to the dreams of others?
And does the father who lives in your dreams
die again when you awaken?
In dream, do plants blossom
and their solemn fruit ripen?

There is a quality of perfection in these dreamy questions. We would not make the slightest move to answer them, or even to respond, although they inevitably cause a cognitive stir. The questions are about motion and becoming, looking backward to the known world, but wondering at its evidence. And each is whole, like an artifact, wrought and concrete, although enigmatic, made by a dreamer's ghostly hand. We might say that they are beautiful examples of what I. A. Richards called "speculative instruments,"[3] both forms of art and forms of mind.

We construct ourselves through such inexplicable forms. Human beings craft their lives through questions; for all of our lives, questions lead our steps. Questions confirm our alliances. Questions frame our trusts. Questions lead our thoughts. As we contemplate them, questions surround our ancestors and our children. We find our way *by* questions; we find our way *into* things; and we find our way *in* things, by asking questions that no one else can ask. As educators, our task is to assist learners to ask the questions that only they can ask, in order to become the strongest, most aware people they are capable of becoming.

Crafting a life through the expression and pursuit of the unknown is a distinctly human task—the crafting of experiences and memories through the pursuit of something we have not seen before, something we cannot fully understand, and perhaps just barely can describe. The museum and the library are workshops for the unfinished questions of others' lives and our own. The educator's workplace lies within the unfinished question that inspires and carries the learner forward. What is happening in there, inside that moment of inquiry? For educators in libraries or museums, that place is our unknown: the learner's unfinished question is something *we* have not seen before, something *we* cannot fully understand, and perhaps just barely can describe. The educator's fitting response emerges from understanding the integrity of such questions and their place in the cognitive night sky we carry with us everywhere.

III

In environments where learners think and act for themselves, the good question is at the center of experience. As a mechanism, even if it is tacit, the good question determines the depth, intensity, and extent of the learner's inquiry and attention. As a discovery, or as a creative act, a good question surprises us and, in a world of speed and motion, will make us pause and refine our thinking.

I have heard the adult educator Alan Knox say that no one learns anything without first having asked a question about it. As much as we may wish to be strong teachers and the sources of authoritative information for learners, I am coming to see that I have not much more to give to my learners than the example of my own questions and how I think of them. Over time in a consistently stimulating environment, I assume that true and useful things will emerge for good learners without my help.

I try to tell my students that my knowledge is always less clear (sometimes pitifully less clear) than I would like, as I ask my questions. I want them to understand that my insights about knowledge and purpose evolve slowly, that they are rarely instant or confident, and they are often lost before I can see them on all sides. I learn things fitfully, episodically, slowly. And even though they may be evanescent, I think that the shaping power of my own best questions and the lessons they imply may outlast all the information I strive to transfer. I tend to live with my questions for a long time. As I say to my students about the ambiguities and tensions we consider together, there are only a few certainties to embrace: No good answer is likely to last very long. Even good answers will change, and they will not be good for everyone.

The good question we look for is more lasting than any answer; it continuously renews us as it leads us on. It is complex: it gently frames our initial cognitive venture in time and space. This grounds us and allows us to ask again from a temporary location, a tabletop to lean on for a moment. Our question aims us generally toward the thing we want to see, to do, to experience, toward our unknown. It tells us when we are near. It slows us and helps us to begin. And then we need some room to let the question settle so we can see it in a different way, in the presence of different evidence.

This is the purpose of the good question: it prepares us for the evidence. If it is a good question, it causes us much trouble. We find that it needs special language to be fully expressed. We find that there is never enough information at hand for us to understand the question fully or to evaluate the information at hand. There is no one to talk to nearby. And, defiantly, a good question will not stand alone for long; parallel or antecedent questions appear, and make their own demands for attention. We assess ourselves and find that our knowledge is inadequate to support even a slim strand of inquiry. We rethink the process. We move toward help, toward information, toward a larger view; if we are learners, we always move in one of these directions; for us, the good question is a polestar.

IV

At times, we ask against the odds. We find that even the most promising question may guide us poorly at first, but unless we abandon it prematurely, lock it inflexibly into only one form, or force it toward an easy answer, a good question can become a valuable thing, a companion to us, and lead us forward through the observations that assist our thinking. Our best questions will teach us patience.

When we frame a new question for ourselves, we take command of our intellectual future. The good question helps to organize the difference we want to make in our knowledge; it is at once a tool, a plan, and an aspiration. Think of the question in three ways.

First, the good question is a guide, a mechanism that allows us to focus, softly as we begin, on an artifact or a text alone, an artifact or a text in an array, an idea, a group of words or sensations given words. The question can assist us to capture our unknown in language, or suggest the possible relationships or theories that might be relevant to knowing something; and these steps begin to construct a context.

Because we have our question in words, we can repeat it to ourselves, revise it, punctuate, and extend it. In the context that is clearest to us (historic, say, or biographic, or geographic) our attention is guided to do its work, which is to begin to shape the unknown by noticing details on our own. Our questions help us to think like historians, biographers, or mapmakers. Because we have a question, we will be better able to recognize something like an answer.

The good question and its unknown are, of course, our own artifacts, malleable, situational, and personal: the good question can be a handmade indicator of the multiple possibilities we have given to ourselves, the *what* and the *if*. When we expand it, a good question may contain countless fragments or variations. Our question is a mechanism with parts, entirely under our design—at least at first. Expanded and made complex, each part of the question offers a possible illumination of whatever object is at hand, and whatever mystery we need to reveal about it to ourselves.

Second, the good question is an instrument of process, because its stability helps us to determine the logics of our approach to the unknown and our initial heuristic in its presence. We can go back to our question and it will remind us of what we wanted at the start of our inquiry, so it is a way to document progress, and how we are moving forward, standing still, slipping back. The question will also help us to make sense of contexts, and to make judgments of utility and relevance.

We ask, What has been brought to our attention that we do not yet fully understand? What are its origins, its organization and structure? What language does it require? How does it differ from the most familiar artifact or idea we already understand? What are the most difficult concepts for me to manage in these observations? Where is the human thing in this object or idea, or in the context that surrounds it? What is the human difference it has made? What knowledge, discovery, process, or skill has brought this into being? What is its meaning in my life? What is its meaning in other lives? How might I make further sense of this? How will this knowledge change my question?

Each of our questions invites information and the discovery of language that further opens the situation and its possibilities. At its best, information and language—flexible, controllable, constructive—will return learners repeatedly to the evidences and contexts at hand, and to the silent concepts beneath the obvious. Every question seriously addressed induces a pause. These operations and their pauses also may permit new structures and dimensions to enter the inquiry: categories, systems, generalizations, cumulations, connections to other objects, and experiences embedded in the warren of memory.

When a logical array of controls and locations is conferred by an intellectual process, the field of inquiry changes. The learner may need vocabulary and reference tools; it may be useful to know the names and contributions of other inquirers and scholars; the original ideas of an artist or innovator may stimulate some new path. Inevitably, appropriate assistance helps to give the inquiry a future beyond the moment, and an understanding of the course a learner might take in the museum, the library or beyond.

The effect of an institution's helping response to a learner's question influences tendencies and techniques for future learning by expanding the learner's controls over processes and tools, whatever further questions may emerge. In this way, the memorable experience of a good question asked in a responsive cultural institution never ends. The good question implies a motion forward, but it also implies a grounding or a building process, with all the lessons and metaphors of construction implied.

Third, after we regard the question as a guide for our attention and as an instrument of process, the question is a tool that we use as we might a hammer or saw: it leads us to build something, to craft more precisely what we want to know, what we want to have happen. The question shapes a structure for us, something we can enter and think within. It also functions as a template when we evaluate new evidence for relevance and fit. The question (like hammer or saw) may be blunt or sharp, but it has an effect we might describe as cognitive craft—shaping, organizing, and storing the matter we collect through our senses and intellect.

To extend the metaphor, it may be best to see the question as a sculptor's tool, or a surgeon's: used with deliberation, it shapes and carves a stone; or it pierces, opening the heart of the unknown so we may see its parts and living energy. Though the tools are simple, these acts are risks. The most naive questions may, in fact, be the most daring, and often have the sharpest steel.

The educative purpose of the cultural institution is *to be there in this process* as both an active presence and a structured situation where critical observations and new questions about experiences can emerge. These observations are critical, because as the tool changes the matter at hand, our observations turn the mind toward new details. They are also empirical observations: we assume that nothing is given to us, except what the learner is able to observe, describe, assess, and then ask again. One question can generate a dozen more questions. Each question can generate countless observations. The more questions we speak aloud, the better. More questions mean more language, and more language initiates more possible connections, and the greater the likelihood that pertinent information will appear nearby. As our spoken questions expand, so do the hidden dimensions of the visible, possible world.

V

In situations where it is possible for human beings to experience, express, and share their own questions as fresh and purposeful—and above all, as their own—the construction of individual, private, and authentic knowledge becomes more real. Great cultural institutions are situations where the learner gives voice to questions, where the learner's experience is a story, where the learner is receptive to advanced connections, and where the learner's cognitive life becomes clearer.

The authentic question cannot be transferred unaltered from one learner to another; a good question belongs originally to its author alone. Nor is a good question likely to disappear. At best, it remains unfinished and resonant in the presence of new experience. The question is renewed when we encounter the right circumstances for asking it again. The question is the artifact of the learner, and there are conditions to this authorship.[4]

The learner is responsible for the learning. The learner controls the economy of the situation, managing the investment of time and attention. A question is always asked from a particular place and perspective, and with a specific idea or construction in mind. Continuity and connectedness flow through the learner's life and into the question. In the delicate balance between continuity and innovation, knowledge is always in change. Consequently, no question is ever asked twice, even by the same learner, using the same language on different occasions. The question is regarded as original in that life: even though it may echo Newton's or Picasso's or Hamlet's question, it is equally the learner's question, possessed in the asking.

Here are observations on some of my own questions. I have begun to review the notebooks and diaries I began in the 1980s when I first undertook my reflections on minds in museums. Among them are many watershed moments that now seem to have meaning primarily in the kinds of questions, and the patterns of questions, I asked then.

Among great treasures, I asked: What is the meaning of the thing itself, as an experience in my own life? What is its meaning in the life of its maker? In my questions, I wanted to grasp the power of the object to open my own memory. I wanted my experience of the object to confirm my own critical intelligence, and by my questions I sought to link it to the experiences of others.

Artifacts from other parts of the world caused me to look for an interior sense of the artifact; I wanted to know it as an object with another life, at a distance from mine. My questions in the presence of the public object were intended to discover the private object, the handmade thing, the tangible outcome of an artisan's life. And every object seems to have moved me toward its original process and purpose: What are the lessons of this thing? What are the lessons of the process, embedded in the object, embedded in its culture? What difference has this made in the world?

Ignorant among scientific and anthropological evidence, I looked for evidences of inquiry and scholarship: How do those who know actually think about this? How has this knowledge been crafted from the evidence? I sought the human context in the fabrication of knowledge through empirical inquiry. The physical anthropologist examines the skull. The geneticist examines the cell. The astronomer gazes at the Hubble image. Here are human beings thinking about evidence, in experiences of mind and order, encountering unknowns. How might I think more like an inquirer here? What is the meaning of this cognitive self-awareness, this mindfulness in the museum? What was the thinking that brought this evidence and knowledge here?

My library notes tell me that I have taken my museum-based questions further. I pursue the meaning of tools and objects in our mental lives: What thoughts do tools make possible? What was a life without metals? In what kinds of cognitive worlds did people dwell before writing, before shelter? What was the difference between a world without containers, baskets, leather pouches, clay jars—and a world with them? What do such vessels make possible? And in this way, in so many ways, my horizon has been defined.

In living history settings, I asked: How does the situation given allow me to reconstruct the minds and concerns of that time? What were the limits of knowledge and constraints on action then?

What information in this life was tacitly given and silently received? Working farm environments would often lead me to questions about my own habitat, so often impractical, isolated and dysfunctional, ahistorical, influenced by people at a distance. Where is the life I see portrayed here, lost in mine? Where is the Shaker, the colonial, the believer, the Union or Confederate regular, the farmer or carpenter I might have been?

In perhaps the most profound and memorable exhibit I have ever seen—a single Wisconsin family's gathering of five generations' artifacts, images, and stories—I asked the most important questions of all, because they continuously returned me to my own family and life: How do such frames of life fit every family? How can these other lives hold moments of my own? What is the legacy of objects and photographs? And I thought of my own dead relations: What is the human frame for my own experience as it was given to me, before I had any choice, other than to accept it? How have I forged this one life from its unwelcome legacies? Among these questions I see in retrospect, there is one question always present, though always unspoken: What is the evidence given here and how can I go beyond it, to make it my own?

To be more specific: During a recent visit I made to the de Menil collection in Houston, I found myself yet again in baffled awe in the Cy Twombly Gallery, asking, What is this large, remarkable chaos? What is the value of these enigmas, these unresolved questions, these encounters with perplexity that never will be clear? In my own life, what is the value of perplexity, the unanswerable question, the unresolvable piece? And then at the Art Institute of Chicago a few weeks later, I felt the same questions with me in the presence of a magnificent collection of Joseph Cornell boxes: What lies hidden behind this transparent tissue of naïveté? What more can I ask of these objects? What response will they offer to me?

Cornell reminds me again of Neruda. Perhaps, as Hayden Carruth said of Neruda's brilliant poem-questions, my own questions (unpoetic, unremarkable, but mine) address the "structure of feeling" underlying my experience.[5]

VI

When I evaluate museums, or when I am present in a cultural institution as an observer with a professional purpose, my observations center on the museum as a forum for the asking of good questions, for the cultivation of invisible processes and original thinking. I look for evidence that tells me the place has high tolerance for the unanswered question, that it appreciates transformative inquiry, and that it makes room for what Barbara Rogoff calls "apprenticeship in thinking."[6] I look for evidence that, when it considers its users, the institution assumes a role in influencing countless individual aspirations and processes of becoming.

Every cultural institution has many ways to think about itself in relation to the "structure of feeling," the energies of inquiry each user carries through the door, embedded and yet engaged in the forward motion of a life. At its best, the museum can be a forum for questions to find expression: a place to express and hear our unknowns among others. At its best, the museum can be an environment where even curators ask their questions in public, as models of thought and inquiry for others.

The institution can also express the high tolerance of scholars for the unanswered, provocative question, the naive and innocent question—and the long periods of ambiguity experienced on any journey toward knowing something worth knowing. It can express its respect for the user whose cognitive or emotional life is most vividly in process, most explicitly unfinished, or even unbegun. At times it is easy to forget that the kind of learning the museum is about is grounded on sensation as well as logic, on inspiration as well as insight. Increasingly, I think it is best understood as the same kind of learning that comes from risking, leaping, and descending; from poetry, music, metaphor, and question, and wish. As Rilke wrote almost a century ago to the young poet, Franz Kappus, "Have patience with everything unresolved in your heart . . . try to love the questions themselves as if they were locked rooms. . . . Live the questions now."[7]

Increasingly, I want to urge us to put all of our assumptions at risk and craft some new possibilities for "living the questions now." Let us go far beyond the idea that an institution can capture, reduce, mark, or measure this imaginative grasping experience; let us not assume that we can describe or fully understand it, apart from noting the stance and the gaze of the learner; and we ought to stop thinking that the transfer of knowledge in the museum here and now matters in any measurable way. A cultural institution is not a school; it is a place where learners ask and consider their own questions, and where the possible resonances are infinite.

For me, that museum that is most educative which is the most suggestive but least compromising, most respectful toward the cognitive powers of the mindful user, and most nurturant of the user's unfinished becoming and unanswered questions. The step forward into that museum happens physically in the world of space and time, but also in mind. It occurs in structures, texts, and contexts, in situations and arrays, but the step forward also happens inside ourselves. There it is surrounded by our expectations, sensations, memories, and hopes. An arrogant response betrays that trust.

VII

We give with our words, our hands, and our minds. We also give with our hearts. What we do as learners and educators in museums, alone or among others, also occurs where we are most private and apart. Just as we know that our behaviors and language are socially apparent and public among strangers, we also know that there are invisible thoughts and invisible actions driving us—and all others—as well. An arrival at either a good question or a fitting response is as much an artifact of imagination as it is a construction of empirical possibility.

People *and* institutions thrive on good questions that do not go away. The words, the contexts, the responses themselves may change, but the unknown remains. When I speak to colleagues,

I urge them to trust with me that the answer to a question is not the point to emphasize in our work. The point is the cognitive motion around the evidence that a question helps us to begin. Of answers, we might assume these things. The best answers are waiting in that motion, and in the inevitable connections that will follow from it. The most complete answers will follow the most persistent and extensive experiences; these will take time. The richest answers will inevitably lead to the construction of more questions. Through one question we may encounter another universe of questions.

The clearest educative purpose of our institution is to illuminate such possibilities in the lives of learners, meaning, of course, also in our own. In the possible: that is where the asking of questions happens, and where our authentic becoming begins.

Notes

An early version of this essay was presented as a keynote address to the Learning in Museums Seminar of the American Association of Museums, at the Museum of the Rockies in Bozeman, Montana, on September 24, 1999.

1. In the December 15, 1995, issue of *The Chronicle of Higher Education*, page B5, a section of the annual report of the president of the Massachusetts Institute of Technology, Charles M. Vest, appeared under the title, "The Pursuit of the Truly Unknown." Rather than list the many achievements of the faculty, Mr. Vest used part of his report to list a sample of the problems that still (in 1995) inspired inquiry and thought. For example:

> "We do not know which classes of earthquakes are predictable. . . . We do not know what the consequences will be for the nation state of the explosion in networked electronic communications. . . . We do not know how we learn and remember, or how we think and communicate. . . . We do not understand the relationship between language and thought. . . . We do not know how viruses form their elegant, geometric structures from commonly occurring protein building blocks, nor do we understand the role of these structures in the infection process."

2. Pablo Neruda, *The Book of Questions*, trans. William O'Daly, (Port Townsend, Wash.: Copper Canyon Press, 1991).

3. I. A. Richards, *Speculative Instruments*, (London: Routledge & Kegan Paul, 1955). See especially the twelfth essay, "Queries" (pp. 133–136), delivered before the Philosophy Department, Harvard University, in October 1945, constructed entirely of questions.

4. These ideas were deeply influenced many years ago by the extraordinary work of Allen Tough, whose insights remain useful. See, for example, *The Adult's Learning Projects: A Fresh Approach to Theory and Practice in Adult Learning* (Toronto: Ontario Institute for Studies in Education, 1979); and *Intentional Changes: A Fresh Approach to Helping People Change* (Chicago: Follett, 1982).

5. William O'Daly, "Introduction," in Neruda, *The Book of Questions*, ix.

6. Barbara Rogoff, *Apprenticeship in Thinking*, (New York: Oxford University Press, 1990).

7. Rainer Maria Rilke, *Letters to a Young Poet*, trans. Stephen Mitchell. (New York: Vintage, 1986), 34.

7

Museums and Public Trust

Consider the museum to be a living cultural trust, a place that holds objects apart and displays them for interpretive engagements by users. It is a place for the private awakenings of thoughtful and constructive people living contemporary lives. As is the case with virtually all engaged institutions—and now, consider beyond the museum, to the hospital, the school, the library—a culture of trust and integrity allows the institution to serve as a credible guide to the complex resonance of things, a resource to embrace for clarity in a complex culture.

The concept of a living trust raises the ideas of ethical practice to the center of every institution and the lives it nourishes. Every professional act in every professional life embodies an interpretation of trust, extending far beyond the letter of the law or the value of the object at hand. To serve in a museum is to serve an ethos of fair and responsible action toward both its collected objects and gathered human beings. These embodied interpretations frame encounters between the collection and its users and provide the culture of learning that gives a character to a cultural setting. An ethic of respect, contextual richness, and generous communication is required to mediate the tensions between chaos and order, between the random and the sequential, between dense complexity and motivated reasoning. This implies an inclusive view of human beings and a desire to assist them in their private tasks.

The museum's public tasks cannot be less than to address knowledge fairly and completely, and in doing so to nourish differences of perception and response. This should involve controversy, alternative interpretations, and emerging points of view. I sometimes argue for the incendiary museum, the museum that ignites passion and engagement; here I suggest that it is a museum's ethical responsibility to do this. One purpose of the museum is, in fact, to enable new points of view to appear, through thoughtful experiences with extraordinary collections. This can happen only in institutions where openness and candor are the rule, and where an impulse to share and explain the richness of knowledge is neither arrogant nor reductive.

A museum organizes a high-profile exhibition of contemporary art. The exhibition earns record amounts of attention and revenue, and it is regarded with critical pleasure. But the museum has failed to disclose that the private collector who loaned the artworks for the exhibition is also funding the show. When this is reported in the press, the perception follows that the museum has allowed the collector to realize likely financial gain from the exhibition. In a single day, it has compromised years of trust it has carefully established with its multiple communities.

As Trudy Govier writes in *Social Trust and Human Communities*, we need each other for knowledge. Present and credible for each other, the museum and its users become "a context of witnesses."[1] Trust is essential in this relationship as the hallmark of cognitive life, because it allows a continuity of constructions and observations from day to day and object to object. Trust allows us to assume a fundamental integrity in the workings of the world, especially among transactions related to learning. These are encounters where we must open ourselves to others and allow ourselves to be led, or at least assisted, in collaborations of trust with people whom Lev Vygotsky (in the context of childhood learning) called "more capable peers."[2]

It is sometimes the very capability and expertise of the museum that leads its users to feel mistrust, or to sense an unbridgeable distance between their entering knowledge and the offerings of the institution. Disengaged from an ethic of collaboration, the remote and powerful museum risks arrogance and false assumptions about its audience. It is always challenged to understand fully the intimate links among the lives of human beings, objects, and information. These are never easy relationships to negotiate or to explain across a diverse and possibly threatened population. And yet this construction of trust is an aspect of ethical service and responsibility to mission that is not merely useful; it is obligatory.

An inner-city museum of history and culture comes to realize that very few people from its own neighborhood visit the museum; consequently, the director and the staff make commitments to carry out an active outreach program, with a particular emphasis on young audiences. After a middle-school group has walked throughout the entire museum, the educator expresses the hope that the students understand this to be a community space, to be visited again and again. There is silence among the students until one says, "The only people in here who look like me are the guards. Why should I feel welcome?"

In my view, the situation of the engaged learner is open, tentative, and vulnerable; we might assume the person to be captive to the acts and insights of becoming, and, in some sense, unfinished and incomplete. The self-determined learner is at least peripherally aware of this and is knowingly dependent on a situation where information, narrative, and involvement all are offered in an environment of trust. From an ethical perspective, the museum is required to cultivate and communicate the values that assist a trusting user: responsibility, fairness, and a long view of the world at hand. For the museum user, a palpable environment of trust and credibility invites the risks of intellectual engagement. For the museum itself, public trust is an artifact of promises made by the institution to inform, communicate, and display with integrity and even courage.

The stakes are not small. The museum is an entity that emanates dense waves of power, value, and authority. It is endowed with power by its treasures, and by its control of knowledge and information. It directs our attention and gives us its objects in galleries, sequences, and patterns over which we have no control. We are given the museum's constructions; we hear its explanations and experience its simulations of context. Our own voices are not particularly important in this relationship—and who is present to listen? However grateful and edified we may feel, from moment to moment in the museum we have very little power over the specific design of our experiences.

When we feel powerless, mere spectators in the museum, an ethical lapse has occurred. I suggest that, just as a museum demonstrates its integrity by how it holds its objects and respects their ownership, there are ethical reasons to regard the user's attention and learning with similar care, if public trust matters to us.

A museum organizes an exhibition of contemporary art by local artists. Among the many works displayed is one that presents multiracial images of the Virgin Mary in modern dress, with bared breasts. Several leaders of the local Christian community are distressed and begin to protest and pray daily outside the museum. Some newspapers and politicians encourage these demonstrations and urge legislators to rescind funding for the museum and dismiss its director and curators. The museum expresses surprise at these expressions of anger and animosity from its neighbors.

Ethical constructions of public work create a structure of trust. This public construction begins with a relatively simple document. The core of an institution's authentic identity is grounded in the strength and clarity of its mission. As an ethical foundation, the mission cannot be overvalued. The mission is a form of contract: it allows a dedication of function, it prescribes a pattern of collection and growth, and it identifies a core curriculum of messages and ideas to be communicated through objects, specimens, and the contexts in which they are shown.

For the user, a mission and its public interpretation are explicit promises made by the well-informed human beings in the institution directly to the presumably less well-informed human beings at the door. When the mission is regarded as a contractual, active, and ethical document, its promises have important potential implications and unspoken parts. *It is our intention to do this*, the promise says. The museum goes on to say,

> We work every day to make our mission happen in the life of our culture, and we work to communicate its content and values to our users and to ourselves.
>
> We collect and hold artifacts and specimens in trust for our users and for the larger human treasury of nature and culture. We also collect and construct information about these examples and we offer it to our users when we are assured of its accuracy, relevance, and fairness.
>
> We display collected objects and texts for users to approach and consider; we create and change the museum as a place for such reflection. We think about museum users, their questions, their learning, and how their experiences here with collected objects might be useful to them. We present objects in contexts, narratives, and histories, and we offer multiple perspectives on them. We respect objects and human beings equally.
>
> Our mission is never complete; our ways of interpreting it are always in change, as knowledge changes and our collections deepen.

Among the public promises made is the assumption that a museum—as an administrative system, as a collector of objects, and as an educator—also has the characteristics of an ethical, reflective, even altruistic actor. The museum asks of itself, "What are the best possible effects of what this institution can do? How might it most usefully develop its collections, teach its users, and influence its cultures? And, in doing so, how might it best fulfill its mission and prosper as an institution?"

No aspect of the museum is immune from the influence of the pervasive mission: not management, curation, education, design, public service, restoration, or preservation. All are challenged to be current and attentive. When the ethical museum is openly embedded in an evolving set of public values and promises, it can better demonstrate a way to understand and address the challenging situations of a contemporary life. The museum has the responsibility to grasp conflicts among scholarly issues and theories and attempt to explain them; but it also must have a credible voice to articulate the tensions of learning we all must resolve by taking risky steps toward the things we do not yet know.

Even in clearly grounded situations, ethical issues are continuously present, continuously creating useful ambiguities for leaders and their institutions. How could it be otherwise? Exigency and the economy often place museums more visibly in the way of cultural dealing and philanthropic self-aggrandizement. Because museums and other cultural institutions often require big money, because they are so often attractive to extravagant sensibilities, and because they frequently seek survival through generous political attention, they are ethically permeable institutions. For a price, they can deliver temporary fame to their benefactors. For alluring flash, they can embrace entertainment at the cost of education. For survival, they can accept gifts, entertain naming opportunities, and glamorize galleries without necessarily addressing the agenda of the institution or extending the reach of its mission. When a gift retains even a slim but venal tether to the ego of the giver, rather than to the giver's generous nature, we have both a problem of ethics and evidence that cultural altruism may be chimerical, something quaint we remember from the last century.

A museum announces the acceptance of a record-setting gift from a wealthy donor who is both politically active and a vocal advocate for

several causes. The gift is so generous that an entire wing of the museum will be renamed. At the announcement ceremony, it becomes clear that the donor anticipates having a hand in determining the exhibits and issues to be featured in the new wing, even though she has no curatorial expertise or relevant professional credentials. The museum's professional staff and its public audiences have the same concern: Has the donor purchased power over the museum's contents and presentations?

It is clear to our professional organizations that venal compromises of mission are inevitably bad for the museum's sense of integrity and purpose and equally damaging to public trust. So complex is our world that its ethical standards are codified, revised, and periodically recodified in great detail and diversity. More than sixty statements are gathered in the American Association of Museums (AAM) publication, *Codes of Ethics and Practice of Interest to Museums*,[3] a volume in its Professional Practice Series. The best of these statements (see, for example, those of the American Association of Museums, the Association of Youth Museums, the AAM Registrars Committee, the Museum Association, and the International Council of Museums) compose a formal structure of mission, obligation, and responsibility. They reflect a level of dedication, character, and care that subtly emerges from the texts. Even the least elaborate ethics codes are direct and sharp in their strictures, almost a set of commandments made robust by their clarity. For example, its members should "Treat all people with civility, avoiding harassment and discrimination," says the Entomological Society of America Ethics Statement. This is simply what is done, the code asserts, we are civil to each other.

A reading of several of these codes suggests that, despite their disciplinary diversity, statements of professional ethics may be reduced to a small number of shared essential guides for behavior, almost completely derived from two principles (articulated here in the ICOM *Code of Professional Ethics*): (1) "Museums are the object of a public trust whose value to the community is in direct proportion to the quality of the service rendered"; and (2) "intellectual ability and professional knowledge are not, in themselves, sufficient, but must be inspired by a high standard of ethical conduct."[4]

Beyond rules and laws, a fundamental professional ethic addresses service to others—and the inspiration of altruism. A review of several codes suggests these ethical consistencies.

- Most codes of professional ethics observe the need to protect the assumptions of trust and regard between an institution and its public. In the most elaborate examples, professional standards are prescribed for virtually all aspects of institutional operations, from assurances of professional credentials, continuing education and training, and currency of practices to the development of diverse audiences. In general, these are what the American Institute of Architects refers to as "a consistent pattern of reasonable care and competence."

- Most codes of professional ethics address standards for acquiring, managing, using, and preserving cultural properties and living collections, showing "informed respect" for their "character and significance" and a moral responsibility for their survival (American Institute for Conservation of Historic and Artistic Works). Within the scope of current knowledge about their care, objects must come to no harm. Accurate, explicit, and current records of collections must be kept. The acquisition, deaccession, and restitution of certain collected objects—particularly human remains, "illicit" traded objects, sacred ritual items, and stolen objects (as in AAM's exemplary *Guidelines Concerning the Unlawful Appropriation of Objects During the Nazi Era*[5])—are frequently addressed specifically, in reference to current international conventions. Among all currently evolving ethical issues, clearly the most serious are those addressing the removal and fair restitution of powerful objects. The most attentive legal and moral reckoning in recent years has demonstrated the power of objects to hold far more than documentary or illustrative powers.

- Most codes of professional ethics urge respect for users, stakeholders, and communities, giving special attention to the voices of individuals and groups and the vulnerability of youth. Codes emphasize attention to services for users with special needs related to ability, literacy, or economics. They also address the physical safety of museum users. Where local community attention is important to museums, the most enlightened codes emphasize provisions for public involvement and inclusion in museum governance and planning as a matter of ethical concern. They articulate commitments to equity and diversity among audiences and staff. The exploitation of individuals or groups is forbidden.

- Most codes of professional ethics urge respect for information and its authenticity, and a "commitment to candor and truth" (American Folklore Society), given to the audience in straightforward ways. Uncredited use or other theft of information, misinformation, and censorship are all forbidden. In the beaconlike words of the American Library Association, "We uphold the principles of intellectual freedom and resist all efforts to censor."[6]

- Similarly, most codes of professional ethics express the primacy of the museum's independent intellectual judgments, uncompromised by the special interests of funders, donors of objects or collections, lenders, political powers, favors, or an array of conflicts of interest. For those affiliated with a museum, grasping personal fortune or power at the cost of the museum or its collections is forbidden. It is common to see ethical statements remind the professional of obligations to the museum profession and its future, to colleagues and peers as well as to the public, and to the pertinent scholarly disciplines of art, history, or science whose knowledge the museum displays.

A trustee of a history museum maintains her own private collection of objects similar to those collected and exhibited by the museum. A rare

object of this kind comes up for sale in another city. The museum bids for the object, but its curator also discovers that he is bidding against the trustee, who wants the object for her own collection. Questions arise about the trustee's use of her position to gain access to museum information and then to establish her own bid. The museum's adminis- trators are concerned that this will become public, to the embarrass- ment of the institution and its trustees.

While codes articulate principles and advice to guide profes- sional behaviors, the real value of an ethic lies beyond the code, in the meeting of obligations and the giving of attention. Codes of behavior cannot, in most situations, be absolute statements: we use them to understand the thin tissues and characteristics of formative trust, interpreting them in specific situations. It is the task of every professional to interpret the ethical code as a living document. The American Association of Museums begins its *Code of Ethics for Museums* [2000] with these words: "Ethical codes evolve in response to changing conditions, values, and ideas"; it goes on to say that a code will "rest upon widely shared values."[7]

As every museum professional knows, cultural settings are part of a living social and intellectual fabric. It is "living" be- cause the lives of users are permeable to the messages and les- sons of the museum's evidence; in consequence, the life of the user becomes different and may continue to change over time. We might say that a newly rewoven living cultural fabric is is- sued from the museum at the end of every visitor's day. There is nothing rule-bound about it.

Similarly, museum work is always a human endeavor, sub- ject to the fluidities of cultural values, social politics, intellectual disciplines, and the evolving bodies of law and practice. All pro- fessional acts—collecting, interpreting, planning—are public in- terpretations of the contract between an institution and its users, a contract grounded in the museum's mission. Throughout the AAM code, the words "mission" and "public trust" are perva- sive, attesting to a fundamental altruism in the institution itself and in its attention to its own integrity. These are not stated in a minor key.

Taken as a whole [the AAM "Code of Ethics" goes on], museum collections and exhibition materials represent the world's natural and cultural common wealth. As stewards of that wealth, museums are compelled to advance an understanding of all natural forms and of the human experience. It is incumbent on museums to be resources for humankind and in all their activities to foster an informed appreciation of the rich and divers world we have inherited. It is incumbent upon them to preserve that inheritance for posterity. . . .

Loyalty to the mission of the museum and to the public it serves is the essence of museum work. . . . Where conflicts of interest arise . . . the duty of loyalty must never be compromised.[8]

The museum's statement of mission is a public expression of promise; therefore, it is an obligation under the care of administrators, trustees, employees, and volunteers. An articulate mission makes clear that all of the museum's work is done in the presence of an obligation to adhere to its aims; therefore, the first criterion of ethical practice is the prominent embodiment of mission in even the smallest of the museum's plans and activities.

There are other criteria as well. As I read it, the AAM code goes beyond the importance of mission by emphasizing the museum professional's responsibility to give attention and service to the common good. Further, professionalism and mutual regard must be present in governance, implying a shared responsibility to consult with others, to assure consistency in decisions, and to evaluate and review as ways to assure a common agenda. Finally, adherence to mission and devotion to the common good forbid personal financial or improper personal gains. The grounding values in the AAM code might be generalized as (1) living up to the public trust, (2) acting for the public good, (3) practicing pluralism, (4) developing diverse audiences, and (5) developing a diverse profession. In this context, the implication of these final three values is that diversity will naturally engender diverse ethical awareness and cultural sensitivity.

An ethical statement is not simply about behaving fairly and keeping objects safe, it is also about actively doing good, presenting and extending authentic and authoritative knowledge, and sustaining an institutional structure that assures both integrity and access. For the museum, an ethic of public trust is not simply useful or decorous; it is obligatory and active every day. It is valuable as a statement of record and as a training document for new professionals. It is at times a procedural document, assuring consistency and fairness. Because it can be renewed and revised, the ethical statement can become an instrument for dialogue, for developing new policies, and for preparing the museum for changes in technology and content. The irony of an ethical code is that it asserts a common moral accord for an entire institution or profession, when in fact it is only by specific, decisive *individual* acts of ethical responsibility that the code is made real. The ethical code is meant to address the personal instrumentality of its agents.

A Holocaust survivor discovers that several handmade silver ritual objects exhibited in a museum may have been stolen from her father, a rabbi, during the Nazi era. The survivor's attorney informs the museum that the provenance of these objects can be documented. The treasures, however, form part of a special collection named for its donor, promised as a gift to the museum. The director and the board are divided in their response to the situation, which may implicate the donor in an illegal purchase or worse. It will certainly compromise the expected donation.

Ethically, what do museums owe to their users? I think it is a pair of inextricable things: responsible museums *first* owe their users intellectual respect, including situations and stimuli for thought and speech, without manipulation or exploitation. *Second*, museums owe their users a whole record of uncompromised evidence, consistent with the limits of mission, constructed fairly and articulated with an impartial and original voice.

There are cultural dimensions of trust, and these affect the will of the user to become engaged by, or subject to, the authority of the museum. Institutions are not always easy to trust. As the array of ethical codes demonstrates, the fabric of trust is complex and requires a step backward to grasp its full scope. A situation of trust implies power, authority, ownership; the museum is invariably in control of the entire situation, including its objects, employees, and physical setting. Trust implies stewardship, the giving of care, the holding of treasures for others, and an agency for the common good, for posterity, and for the use of learners. This implies conservation, preservation, and limited access, meeting the responsibility of the museum to keep objects safe from physical damage. But the object, if it is to be kept at all, must hold something more, and that, too, is protected and preserved by the stewardship of the museum.

Trust, as I want to speak of it here, implies aspects of the invisible and the unspoken surrounding the object: memory, sacredness, continuity, legacy, and belief, depending on whatever the object may have meant originally. We might think of these contexts as collected strands of place, authorship, discovery, use, rarity, exquisiteness, or value, information derived from research, observation, and scholarship. In this aspect, trust implies the crafting and keeping of truth insofar as it can be known; we trust that the museum has fabricated nothing to mislead us. Trust also implies the impulse to think and act for the good of another, or for the common good, and for the good of the institution. To trust in an institution also will mean trust for its independence of action and judgment: for example, we are likely to value a public library in part because it is guided by a pervasive ethos of access to information and dedication to a community of users. It exists only for us as a community and only for our use. Finally, the idea of trust also implies the presence of conscience, of rigorous processes of review and attention to trust itself. The trustworthy institution monitors its processes to assure compliance with law, mission, and the professional ethics of the field.

But as we must speak of it, trust is an aspect of professionalism that extends beyond the law; its presence makes social exchange possible. Bernard Barber, in *The Logic and Limits of Trust*, describes the value of trust for its "general function of social ordering, of providing cognitive and moral expectational maps for actors and systems as they continuously interact."[9] Barber defines "professional roles and behavior in terms of three essential variables, each somewhat independent of the others: powerful knowledge, considerable autonomy, and a high level of fiduciary obligation and responsibility both to individual clients and to the public welfare."[10] It is the idea of "fiduciary obligation" that moves trust beyond the legal into the moral realm of our work. Barber writes that this idea entails "the expectation that some others in our social relationships have moral obligations and responsibility to demonstrate a special concern for other's interests above their own. . . . Trust as fiduciary obligation goes beyond technically competent performance to the moral dimension of interaction," especially in regard to the use of knowledge from a position of power.[11]

The director of an important museum suddenly resigns from his post. In the interim, the chairman of the museum board takes over the director's daily tasks. The search for a replacement takes many months. The museum staff is shocked to read in the press that the board chair has paid himself a generous, six-figure salary for his period of service as acting director, despite the voluntary nature of the board chairmanship.

Barber suggests that, as professionalism increases, so do the appearances of the three variables—knowledge, autonomy, and fiduciary responsibility. Further, it is not difficult to see how increases in the first two will demand increases in the third. Instances of "powerful knowledge" in museums are impossible to count in all of their forms. Consider briefly the museum's collections of expertise: the expanses of collection development, the depths of curatorial expertise, systematic classification, conservation technology, educational programming, management, planning, and finance—and the countless examples of scholarly empirical contributions to the historic, aesthetic, social, and scientific record.

The museum professional is also the owner of significant autonomy in selection, design, construction, display, narration, and evaluation of the museum's work. No principled museum professional will easily accept a donor's strings, or other controlling attachments, no matter how grand the gift. The third of Barber's elements—the professional's fiduciary responsibility—is the essential element in the construction of trust and obligation for the museum. The ethical museum professional rigorously observes the institution's obligatory trust to objects and living collections, to the development of knowledge, and the exercise of values. But beyond this, trust also entails the provision of direct service to the culture of museum users, in whose collective name the institution's treasures are kept.

What are the enemies of public trust? Here is my brief list.

Unfairly derived assumptions about the museum's users.

- Failure to evaluate and revise exhibitions to assure accuracy and currency
- Failure to converse with museum users before and after planning and during installation
- Failure to understand differences among audiences and to explore these differences
- Failure to consult and engage stakeholders in the museum's communities

Failure to present issues of ethics, and other social, intellectual, and situational complexities in public.

- Such as attempts by authorities to censor exhibitions
- Such as attempts by authorities to politicize exhibitions
- Such as attempts by authorities to abridge professional independence
- Such as attempts by collectors to manipulate demand and pricing

Failure to express the complex moral life of an institution.

- In cases of objects seized or stolen
- In cases of sacred objects and human remains
- In cases of controversial scholarly interpretations
- In cases of tensions between mission and marketplace

Failure to arrive at a broad accord of what ethical behavior entails.

- In relation to the inanimate object or the living organism
- In relation to the professional lives within the institution
- In relation to the diverse community of users and learners
- In relation to corporations and commercial interests
- In relation to donors

A museum is a way of making and connecting knowledge, and, as in any setting of record, an invisible structure of testimony stands behind its evidence: a record of inquiry, research, scholarship, insight, exploration, documentation, and reflection. In her work on social trust, Trudy Govier writes, "Knowledge based on testimony is absolutely fundamental."[12] In her words, we need each other for knowledge. "Our constructed view of the world depends on many other people, and we can discover what these other people have experienced and what they judge to be the case only because we generally believe their testimony."[13]

The crafting of truth depends on trusting the testimony of many others, and, by extension, it entails an assumption of trust in what others have crafted for themselves. "We place our trust in that intersubjective account, thereby presuming honesty, competence, and reliability on the part of the people and social institutions who define it. Truth," Govier writes, "presumes trust."

A person who seeks to ignore intersubjective beliefs and standards will stand isolated from the life of others and the knowledge and practices of the community. Acknowledging and accepting intersubjective truth means relying on the processing of information done by other people. Some will be strangers to us, yet we have to rely on them when we stand within public systems of knowledge and belief. Systems and institutions provide knowledge and authority; people collaborate and must trust each other to define truth. To define truth together, we have to have confidence in each other.[14]

For Govier, there is no other way to craft personal knowledge.

We may best understand testimony from its common legal associations: it is delivered in a formal context, where qualifications, competency, interrogation, limits of expertise, and proximity to relevant evidence are established by precedents and practices. In cultural institutions, the testimonies offered as truth have similar claims. By expertise and experience with evidence, the museum asserts membership in an epistemic community. Oral and written testimony surround and contextualize the evidence of objects and specimens themselves. Standing often on the shoulders of giants, the museum constructs objective order, expresses informed perceptions, specifies differences among details, and asserts the best knowledge it can in the public space it occupies. More than in any other institution, the construction of knowledge in the museum depends on collaborative trust; in some ways, the testimony of the museum is incomplete until its audience hears it. Govier writes, "Human beings may think individually as well as in dialogue, but we seek to confirm our thoughts, our words and reasonings about the world, together with other people. To do so we must listen to each other and, when appropriate, believe each other. To be able to do so, we must learn from each other."[15]

The museum is an incomparable setting for the construction of knowledge based on what Govier calls "reflective trust," a process that follows not from innocence or automatic acceptance, but from comparisons with the knowledge we carry, the sorting of complexities, and the use of critical thinking skills. "From another person we gain vicarious access to the world; we can acquire beliefs or knowledge based on experience we do not have ourselves. Reflective trust is likely to be qualified, partial, and context dependent. But it is still trust."[16]

In the processes of independent learning, dependence on the testimony and evidence of others is entirely fitting, and entirely necessary. For an inquirer of integrity, the critical processes of thought involved in the discovery and taking-in of evidence are difficult to compromise. The learner in the museum is driven by questions, by steady judgments of relevance and coherence, by attention to discrepancy and variation. The great museum is constructed exactly for this process. Rigorous reflective thinking in the museum is likely to be proportionate to the level of reflective trust the institution evokes.

But, as our ethical codes make clear, none of this can happen by accident. As a living public trust, the museum must be vigilant to preserve its integrity from arrogance, censorship, fanaticism, and exploitation. Toward this, I suggest that four ethical aims should be considered, debated, and perhaps embraced; they will be familiar to any ethically sensitive observer of cultural institutions.

> *Transparency of processes.* Every museum should strive to make the elements of its work clearer by accompanying an exhibition with statements about its origins and intentions, its challenges and surprises, and its relationship to mission and the transmission of knowledge. Beyond intellect and scholarship, particularly when its objects are potentially controversial or provocative, an exhibition is the product of genius and courage. These dimensions deserve display and debate. Any reduction in mystery helps to illuminate the invisible structure and institutional energy that brings brilliant objects and ideas into place.
>
> *Multiple approaches to evidence.* Any scholarly arena will readily acknowledge that there are multiple intellectual ways to contemplate evidence and that our truths are crafted privately by combining and recombining our experiences with the experiences of others. Therefore, it is evidence of ethical respect for the user to provide multiple models of response to an object or an entire exhibition and the problems it responds to. It is useful, in fact, to present the museum and its collections as a response to a problem of knowledge, a gathering of evidence, and a presentation

of testimony that continues to be constructed. Cultural institutions ought to acknowledge that they address unfinished issues in human culture and individual lives.

Authorship and an author's voice. The idea of testimony implies a specific source of expert opinion, an individual approach to the relevant matter at hand. So it is useful for the museum to overcome the anonymous museum voice by citing the authors of museum scholarship, noting collaborators, and presenting the museum's work as a model of human inquiry, conducted for public display. Present the exhibition as a synthesis of previous scholarship and new insights based on the assembled objects. The institution cannot easily be a model of thought; the individual human being *thinking* can be such an exemplar.

Models for independent critical thinking. Every museum owes its users an opportunity to think beyond the museum, to make judgments of their own. Toward this, every museum should pose and illuminate questions that are inherently difficult to address. Such questions may be taken back to the galleries to provoke new observations, or as easily carried into the everyday spaces that follow the museum experience.

The adjective "living"—as in "living trust"—suggests that the pertinent attributes of the museum should be analogous to those of an ideal user, a person who is driven equally by curiosity, fair vision, and engagement with knowledge. As a living public trust, the bold museum will enact a public contract with its communities and funders, assuring active principles of fairness, multiple approaches to knowledge, and attention to the reflective trust of learners. Critical thinking on the part of all stakeholders is pertinent to enacting this public contract. Over time, media, politics, violence, and abuse may have compromised or deeply damaged our ability to trust in altruism and assume institutional good will. In a culture of cascading change and altered boundaries, what are the needs and purposes of trust? What causes an evolution of trustworthy practice? What defines or alters an ethical code? How much should ethical values evolve, and how do they change?

In this new millennium, pervasive tensions and constraints may mean that our cultural institutions operate under new and potentially compromising circumstances. From my perspective, I wonder about the effects of these things on our cultural and intellectual lives.

- Information is widely accessible, but has no boundaries, variable authority, and few opportunities for control
- Entertainment tends to drive content
- Economics and politics can hold cultural institutions hostage, compromising their independence
- Leadership and fundraising are not simply coincidental but integral and easily confounded
- Learning and testing have become synonymous, and other forms of reductive accountability have become appealing forms of evidence

The changes wrought on information, social, and educational accountability, the situation of youth, the shallow realm of public entertainment, and the coherence of communities are themselves likely topics for all museums to consider in their work; none of them is above these conditions. An ethical museum in a future of tensions recognizes that, in the words of the Dalai Lama, "the interests of a particular community can no longer be considered to lie within the confines of its own boundaries."[17]

In this world, the great and ethically sensitive museum will present itself as *thinking*, making choices, expressing reasons for its content and what it collects, asking questions about the processes of understanding, and describing museum practices and contexts. This museum will address the intellectual and situational complexities of experiencing and using a museum; it will recognize the challenges it presents to users and assist them to become active learners. The voices of users will be heard in the museum; the museum will examine its patterns of use, conduct empirical research with its audiences, and involve observations of previous patterns in future planning, content, and design.

I believe that we act ethically in our professions because ethical acts move us forward, toward others, in order to create together a fabric of effects on the world we have chosen and then individually crafted as our own. The rigor of our scholarship and the depth of our good intentions may be far less important to the credibility of the museum as an institution than the depth of our altruism. We find an essential integrity when we build a collection that becomes more than its parts; when we conduct deep research toward the very best information possible; when we exhibit works of knowledge, genius, and art; and when we educate a public so that it might think in new ways. But we should recognize, as well, that all of our effects on other human beings depend on the authenticity of our words and acts, on our respect for others, and on our disciplined adherence to our mission. These are promises made, to be lived out in our lives and the lives of our institutions.

Notes

A version of this essay appeared in the September/October 2001 issue of *Museum News*, the bimonthly magazine of the American Association of Museums.

1. Trudy Govier, *Social Trust and Human Communities* (Montreal & Kingston: McGill-Queen's University Press, 1997), 56.

2. Lev S. Vygotsky, *Mind in Society: The Development of Higher Psychological Processes*, ed. Michael Cole et al. (Cambridge, Mass.: Harvard University Press, 1978), 86.

3. *Codes of Ethics and Practice of Interest to Museums*, comp. Jackie Weisz (Washington, D.C.: American Association of Museums, 2000). All quotations from codes of ethics are taken from this compilation.

4. *Codes of Ethics*, 204.

5. *Guidelines Concerning the Unlawful Appropriation of Objects During the Nazi Era*, (Washington, D.C.: American Association of Museums, 1999 [amended 2001]).

6. In addition to the American Library Association's *Code of Ethics*, see also its statements, *The Library Bill of Rights* and *Libraries: An American*

Value. These and other documents related to intellectual freedom are available at the website for ALA's Office of Intellectual Freedom <http:www.ala.org/alaorg/oif>.

7. *Code of Ethics for Museums* (Washington, D.C.: American Association of Museums, 2000), 2.

8. *Code of Ethics for Museums*, 3–4.

9. Bernard Barber, *The Logic and Limits of Trust* (New Brunswick, N.J.: Rutgers University Press, 1983), 19.

10. Barber, *The Logic and Limits of Trust*, 135–136.

11. Barber, *The Logic and Limits of Trust*, 14–15.

12. Govier, *Social Trust*, 59.

13. Govier, *Social Trust*, 61.

14. Govier, *Social Trust*, 62.

15. Govier, *Social Trust*, 60.

16. Govier, *Social Trust*, 69.

17. His Holiness the Dalai Lama, *Ethics for a New Millennium* (New York: Riverhead Books, 1999), 165.

8

Crafted Truths: Respecting Children in Museums

I

In the same way that play is not about toys, the child's museum is not about objects. It is about the invisible actions of consciousness and instrumentality, the child striving to construct the possibilities of one life within the limits of childhood. How to think about and design an experience. How to express and understand its possible dimensions. And then, how to change these dimensions and take control of them. This is *becoming*, no easy work.

In the same ways that participating in grand life events transforms youth into maturity by giving depth and resonance, the museum can be an important cognitive event in the life of the child, if the museum's systems, objects, tools, and human interactions all intend to make new thinking not only possible but completely necessary in order to participate.

It is important to respect and preserve the integrity of the museum as an inviting institution grounded on objects, inquiry, and knowledge. It is equally important to respect and preserve the integrity of the child as a thoughtful being. Every person, child or adult, brings a complex life grounded on experience, language, and memory to the museum. Every mind there, child or adult, is on the edge of expectation, hope, and insight.

What children see, feel, and understand in museums contributes to a continuously expanding cognitive record that becomes richer and more complex over the lifespan. Not only do strong images and engaging information become permanent parts of our repertoires of memory, these images and information help us to reinterpret what we have seen and known in the past. Museums move us forward.

This is the steady motion of minds in museums: Our unanswered questions awaken; we are moved to ask them again; we reinvent them in new forms. Or, astonished, we ask entirely new questions. We always seek fresh answers, even if they are incomplete, even if they raise more difficult questions.

It is a difficult but essential challenge for the museum to translate depth of knowledge, care, and responsibility surrounding its collections into an effective alliance with the mind and instrumentality of the child. To evaluate this alliance, every museum needs to reconsider its own understanding of what museums are supposed to do, and what it assumes children in the museum to be, or better, what it is that the museum will assist them to become.

What stance does the museum take toward the children who enter it? Are they students, learners, thinkers, problem solvers? What are young users given in the museum to confirm that identity, *learner*? How are they assisted?What are they given to reflect on? What problems are they offered to solve? What evidence and tools are present? What reasoning is possible? Where might the reasoning lead?

Are children in the museum understood to be receivers of information or discoverers of information? Are they waiting for direction or striving to break away? Do children enter the museum with their own goals, independent of the goals of others? Do children have opportunities to select and have experiences of their own, on their own? Does a child in the museum have an opportunity to be an independent learner? In what ways can the experiences of children in the museum be combined to illuminate each other? Do children carry museum observations into their homes and communities or into other contexts that continue outside the museum? What does the museum want to have happen to children? What might happen tomorrow as a result of experiences today?

I don't think of these as purely rhetorical questions, but as ways to remind the museum that its assumptions can be instructive. Does the museum pose any great, continuously open questions to children? Do children see and hear adults grappling with things they don't yet understand? Is knowledge suggested as a process rather than an end?

Here are some other questions I apply when I observe in museums, to understand the qualities of thought that support the structure and situation given to users, regardless of age.

- How much information is given to the learner as part of the museum experience? Does this information provoke questions? Does the situation invite speculation and hypothesizing? Does it imply ambiguity and complexity to be explored, and does it lead the user toward immersion in a problem or experience?

- Does the situation offer a story, a narrative that contains cultural realities, connections to experiences, contexts of time and human understanding? Is the story connected to an identifiable person, hero, scholar, leader, or researcher? Are we helped to understand that person's situation, perspectives, challenges, and thoughts?

- Are unfinished parts of knowledge present? Does the situation encourage the user to finish the situation by acting, speaking, or reasoning? Does the situation inspire cooperation with another person?

- Are users encouraged to talk to others, to make original observations, or to document something for themselves— use a book or an information tool, for example, or take away an idea to pursue tomorrow?

- Does the museum discuss research and scholarship about its subject matter, so that users know that knowledge is continuously increasing, and that real people make knowledge happen? Does the museum's own community of knowledge—its curators, naturalists, or educators—appear to museum users in some predictable, accessible form, talking about their work?

- Are there moments in the children's museum that address adults, helping them understand the experience of the child and their own educative relationships with the child? Does the museum assist the adult to act for the child's own experience and to disencumber the child from fear or hesitation? Does the museum have ways of transforming an adult to become a companion in the experience of the child?

- Does the museum experience have a future? Does it make possible new thoughts outside the museum? Does it suggest situations in the usual experience of everyday life where a memory of the museum might be appropriate, or even illuminating? That is, does the museum cause itself to be thought about afterward?

I am looking for museum situations that create opportunities for their users to become different people: museums that require a pause for clarity, that want to stimulate mindful exchanges and actions, that involve transmissions between human beings, and that offer genuine unknowns and vivid memories. I am looking for a museum that understands that its most important work occurs beyond objects. I am looking for the museum that encourages children to make useful errors and that acknowledges adult errors. And I ask, last, does the museum show how new knowledge is untidy and often unpredictable, visual, and imaginative—and how it changes the knower?

In contrast to many popular conceptions of childhood, I think it is important to cast children and museums in a somewhat less than magical and imagination-soaked light. Museums are not always rhapsodic events in the lives of children. I suspect that they are often overmanaged and unsatisfying experiences. For many children, they may be excessively intense, charged with promises and expectations. They should not be thoughtless entertainment, but surprising encounters with new ideas and roles.

For many children, museums can provide experiences of intensity, hope, and intellect. They are places of engaging work in observation and documentation. They involve purposeful, empirical, imaginative, grounded, and ordinary and extraordinary thinking. They present circumstances of intrigue and curiosity. They entail public and private questionings, comparable to serious adult inquiry. They may involve dialogue with companions and further experiences of language. They may lead to writing and reading, to seeking documents and additional information. They may lead to further pursuits beyond the museum and its constraints, among other objects and texts, and other lives.

It might be useful to describe the museum user's tasks not as opportunities for learning or education, but as moments or situations for new thoughts. All learners should be helped to know the constructive play of such moments. For children, they are also opportunities to be with caring adults and other children outside the home, engaged in a traveling conversation, moving through the setting as a single unit: a moving conversation with legs, heads, hands, and eyes. The best work of the individual child in the museum is to use these moments of combination and shared energy for thinking well, asking questions, seeking information, and taking pleasure in the senses invited by new images of possibility. It is less important to learn in these moments than it is to feel capable and engaged and to take pleasure as well in not being alone.

The best and most complex moments I experience in thinking about museums are those moments that overturn my expectations and renovate my convictions. Even though I have been able to forge my perspective over two decades in all kinds of museums, it is in museums for children and youth that my understanding has done the most turning over.

In these museums I see situations where children are able to give direct attention to their own becoming through experiences of thought, attention, and communication. These museums assist their users to live in and to experience their own instrumentality, as they express interest, form questions, or in deep pauses, are seized by possibilities. Here are the museum's most educative gifts, moments for the crafting of one's own truths and for taking critical steps toward leading a self-determined life.

These elements in children's museums—the child in space and time, the mind in motion among possibilities—have led me to believe that museums of all kinds are less about objects than they are about the construction of ideas, processes, and contexts; that what museums offer as the *known* is often surrounded by a more inviting *unknown*, by ambiguities and great questions. It is also clear to me that museum users use the museum best when they are thinking, reasoning, and communicating, and that the museum is less for *receiving* and more for *crafting* experiences and understandings of the world. It is less about magic than it is about artful logic, and this is a good thing; learning is not based on illusions but on a person's discoveries, on personal terms.

I think it is useful to develop caution when we talk about *learning* or *education* in museums, because those two words are deeply and inevitably entwined with what we may think should happen in schools. I have, over time, sought to stop using the words *museum learning* and *museum education*, and have tried to substitute a couple of others, though it does not always work. Generally, I try to refer to *useful museum behaviors* or *vivid museum experiences* or *cognition in the museum* or *critical thinking in the museum*, when I want to talk about the effects of museum use on an individual mind. It is the mind of a *user*, not a visitor.

These somewhat awkward words are not merely ceremonial or symbolic terms; rather, they move me closer to the things I want to see happening in museums, things we all require a new vocabulary for:

Useful museum behaviors are acts that move museum users forward toward their own insights, such as pausing to think through new information, or to write something down, to converse with a companion, or to ask a question out loud, or to repeat an action in order to feel it again.

Vivid museum experiences are the ones made memorable by the confluence of object, space, time, and human being—a momentary flicker of memory made new, or a sustained peak experience in the presence of insight, or a single transforming piece of information.

The idea of *cognition in the museum*—or perhaps the better, more lively term is the word used by Ellen J. Langer, *mindfulness*[1]—carries with it the idea of moving several steps beyond merely processing data about objects, to the understanding of contexts and relevance, and to active reflections about other experiences with similar objects, and perhaps to the revolutionary implications of new data.

This is, of course, not far from the essence of *critical thinking*, a term that we may always find difficult to define, but which we will know when we see it working. That is, when we encounter in the museum any one of the following mental operations, taken from a longer list in Frank Smith's wonderful book, *To Think*.[2] I have selected them from Smith's larger lists because they seem most likely to appear in museum contexts, when users are in the presence of challenging objects or are stimulated by unexpected questions.

clarifying	*discriminating*	*identifying*	*searching*
classifying	*distinguishing*	*interpreting*	*seeking*
comparing	*evaluating*	*judging*	*being skeptical*
conceptualizing	*examining*	*matching*	*stating*
detecting	*finding*	*questioning*	*verifying*
differentiating	*grasping*	*recognizing*	*weighing evidence*

There are obviously many more terms that may occur easily to us. It is not revolutionary to suggest that, whether the museum invites them or not, these mental acts will occur as a matter of awareness and because we require new thoughts to live a forward life. It seems to me that, if allowed to manage our own cognitive lives, human beings will naturally do a fair job of giving themselves cognitive problems: clarifying, comparing, evaluating, interpreting objects, and judging, stating, weighing evidence about objects—these are the cognitions that define our minds and give meaning to our acts. "We are problem-solvers by nature," John W. Gardner has written, "problem-seekers, problem-requirers."[3]

In association with critical thinking about objects, it may be useful to suggest yet another phrase to replace "museum learning," and that is *quality of thought in the museum.* Smith also provides a list of the concepts likely to be affected by a critically thinking person's engaged mind; they are the critical subjectivities of thought.[4]

accuracy	*data*	*information*	*relationships*
ambiguity	*definitions*	*knowledge*	*relevance*
authority	*differences*	*observations*	*similarities*
clichés	*evidence*	*patterns*	*statements*
clues	*facts*	*problems*	*strategies*
criteria	*generalizations*	*reasons*	*theory*

We attend to these things and use them to document what our senses grasp without language.

Invited to strive, to move forward by thinking, museum users are engaged in provocative experiences. We must be interested in the future of these moments, and the power of the museum to sustain them.

Consequently, I think the tasks of the museum for children are to create convivial situations for thinking, to inspire responses to questions and issues, and to offer informing evidence. This means assisting children to manage the cognitive challenges in the environment and supporting the array of behaviors that lead toward memories and cognitive changes. Useful questions cannot be disassociated from their authors; the museum can help the child to ask and nurture something personal and interesting. And, in the presence of objects and ideas, the museum ought to offer an invitation that says, "It is possible to think further about this. You must think further about this," as it simultaneously offers the message, "You are strong enough to know more, and to ask and follow your own questions. The museum can help you to do this."

After believing for years that it might be possible to master the principles and contexts of museum learning, I have come to see that it seems too diffuse and complex an activity to understand fully in any museum, in any person. It is probably more accurate to assume that museum experiences comprise an infinite constellation of responsive and reflective behaviors, different for each individual, innumerable, and changing moment by moment, in different stimulating situations.

And so we might better think of *cognition, awareness,* or *critical thinking,* rather than *learning.* When people use museums—for reflection and diversion, for dedicated contemplation, for conversations and explorations with objects—they expand their repertoires of experience and cognition. They construct a memorable image or phrase; they connect the present with the past; they hypothesize. Perhaps this is learning, but naming it does not matter very much to me any longer.

The problem of any museum user is a problem of thought, and it is the same problem that people have everywhere when they read or talk, experience the media, or work in classrooms: How do I think critically in the presence of new information? How do I behave in the presence of an unknown? The museum's problem is also connected to thought: how to be a place where human change occurs through thoughts and stories, nurtured by objects, information, and the presence of other human beings?

To be a place where change occurs for children, the museum should lead its young users toward new interpretive possibilities and individual observations, emphasizing alternate readings of objects and lives. Every object and every life has multiple frames; every object and every life needs its own language. The museum should be an occasion for talk about stuff without limit. No one lives in the museum, isolated from peers or others. And so, unless the museum constantly refers to the world beyond itself, the world where human beings live and act, it will not lead the user to think beyond the immediate experience; that is, to think *into* the world.

Thinking enhances exploration among rich connections and it helps to balance awe. A museum's structural logic and connections to the everyday do not diminish its exploratory richness;

rather, they increase the magnitude of possible insights and connections a learner can make. The museum needs to balance awe and logic, inclining at times toward describing mysteries and unknowns, and how others have thought about them. Museum logics and information structures offer children the possibilities of systematic cognitive change in the midst of unknowns, through naturally exploratory and dedicated thought. As experienced in a museum, the magic might take the form of "things to wonder about," "unfinished thoughts," or "ideas to pursue."

The possibilities of the museum also might take the form of ordinary life stories of people who become thoughtful, smart, generous, and graceful, by growing up feeling strong and able. We need narratives of thoughtful, problem solving people, speaking in their own voices, describing what they are working on and what they hope to know. Individuals and groups who address something outside themselves with implications for other lives will always offer lessons to learn. Every cultural institution must be challenged to address the living world nearby.

A museum is a cultural institution, not only because it displays cultural artifacts, but also because it is derived from and extends the culture that sustains it. Our museums are excellent at presenting the logics of natural and scientific processes that explain evolution and order in the universe, the workings of machines and mechanical systems, the settlements of the frontier, and the histories of great occasions.

But museums are not very good at conveying what I think of as the transforming processes of human life. By this I mean negotiating the difficult social and emotional prospect of growth into one life as it matures; understanding the extensions and powers of that life to do oneself good and ill; becoming an able communicator in a noisy environment; and being able to sort out values and prospects—and understand which to follow, which to change, which to share with others. The elusive processes I most care about are thinking, reflecting, keeping silent in order to work out next steps, grasping the point, dealing with reorganizing insights, and finally speaking our thoughts out loud in order to become their champion in dialogue.

Increasingly, I want to see museums take as their cause the stimulation of courage, self-confidence, compassion, and authentic participation in life.

In museums I am most interested in everything that is not an object, the immaterial among the material: the experiences offered, the words heard and seen, the messages invoked by an environment, the nature of problems explored, the information given, the information not given, the possibilities of interacting usefully and building relationships, encouragements to mindful actions, and new explanations of puzzling things. I think I am also most interested in the unknowns the museum acknowledges, the things one may be urged to find out for oneself, with the tools and information given. Perhaps this is why I want to replace the idea of the museum *visit* with the implications of museum *use*.

What I hope to see and understand in the future children's museum is how our culture constructs childhood as an experience of thought. While the museum offers things for children to touch, experiences to remember, devices to work, objects to see, opportunities to wonder, I want to know what it offers for children to think about: problems to solve, mysteries to contemplate, unfinished issues to work on over a lifespan.

The future youth museum is less about explaining objects than it is about giving form to the logics of discovery and knowledge—including the cultures and processes of arts, social sciences, sciences, and information. The human task is to go well beyond the stuff and the technology, to capture the experiences and information that reconstruct the diverse dramas of one culture, and to tell how its leading thinkers, scientists, artists, authors, and activists work.

The museum is an environment that can keep its promises to children by offering experiences without the risks and judgments of the classroom. For both adult and child, there is the need to overcome the experiences of schools, where the overmanaged dimensions of interaction are often obstacles to true engagement. Learning is mixed with so many other functions in school; to me, it is often compromised as a purpose. A thoughtful museum offers different kinds of rewards and unusual qualities of safety. If one hears the voices of many children correctly, the school cannot keep promises of this kind, so it is seen as an environment without integrity, and worse, without possibility, or without trust.

Authenticity is a form of action: the authentic museum is a place for helping experiences to occur, not simply for consuming experiences as they are given.

For every child, the museum ought to be an opportunity to renegotiate the meanings of his or her place in the culture at hand—and to glimpse a differently informed future. For the child who is strong, it is an opportunity to build and question, question and build what one knows. But for the child who, in the presence of information and complexity, thinks first of fear, the future museum ought to be an opportunity to test one's strength, and to find out, in Jules Henry's words, that "I may be stronger than I think."[5] For the child who is lost or who feels lost, the museum can offer continuities and connections between herself or himself and the rest of the world.

II

I believe that people should come to cultural institutions with hope, expectation, and need, drawn by the possibility or desire to change through informed experiences. Families should come to museums to become better families—more attentive to each others' differences, more communicative, better prepared to pause and pay attention to one another. Individuals should come to museums to become better at understanding themselves and making new sense out of what they think.

It is important to consider the children's museum as a cognitive space, consisting of a thinking child, alone or in a group of caring others, in a place where reflection, communication, and experience are assisted consciously, and where the child is always stronger, more independent as a learner, for being present.

Unless something thoughtful and important follows from museum use, there is no value to it. There are many challenges to this: Does the museum fortify and extend its alliances with schools and libraries? Does the museum intentionally seek to undo the mindlessness of television and radio? Does the museum specifically strive to ease the tensions of children's lives?

What do we want to have happen? I think the future museum ought to forge a present and future advocacy for the child. Here are ten possible goals in the development of this future museum.

- For every child, as for every adult, the museum should become a trustworthy environment where fear is given limits, while thought is unlimited. It should be a place where the child, like the adult, is treated as an independent learner, able to participate fully in selecting and constructing experiences, discovering and lingering over a particularly rewarding experience.

- The museum might also become for the child, as it also can become for the adult, the central community institution among the web of all lifelong institutions that shape and engage the power to think critically and intensely over time, in order to live a knowing life in a material world. Like the library, the museum must be understood as a place where free inquiry happens.

- The museum should be the primary setting where children can come to understand more about the operations of other institutions in the world—from the local hospital to the European Economic Community to the public schools in Tokyo—and to see themselves and others as individuals with interests and futures shared community-wide and worldwide.

- A great museum will capture its culture and reflect its inevitable diversity to the entire community of users. There are data to be shown: demographics, institutions, schools, libraries, zoos and gardens, historic buildings, media, academic centers, religious bodies, corporations—as well as particular descriptions and images of a community's generations. Everything in the museum should say these comforting words: you are here.

- The adult's experience in the child's museum ought to be a learner's experience as well. One way that adults grow up is by coming to understand the complex situations—intellectual, personal, physical—of their children. It is useful for all adults to remember at times the tensions and vulnerabilities of their own childhoods.

- In general, growing up ought to be encouraged for everyone: it is a good thing to do, Peter Pan and Walt Disney notwithstanding. Perhaps the museum is the primary institution able to argue against the infantilization of our culture, while speaking up for the value of useful and satisfying play.

- And just as we should help children to think favorably and comfortably about themselves, we may have the same goals for parents. We should help them to think about their relationships to children, to see how language affects feelings and to see what qualities, over time, create families defined by mutual trust.

- The children's museum should be explicit about helping parents to learn the ways that families can themselves become trustworthy environments where all fears are given limits, especially fear of failure, while thoughts themselves, especially thoughts of possibility, are unlimited.

- Children need a museum that is also a forum for their voices.

- The museum is the ideal institution to help children understand the great themes of living one's life: do useful and good work; be generous to others and oneself; understand and emulate heroes; attend to others; grasp and value human differences. These themes are founded in childhood; they come early in life and they last long.

- We might usefully pay attention to the child's need to understand the great facts of difference and change as they appear in our culture, especially those involving technology, politics, economics, privacy, health, and human diversity (ethnicity, culture, religion). If children can attend to the social dimensions surrounding our lives, they may be able to anticipate and leap ahead of them, rather than begin with inadequate knowledge and never catch up.

These suggestions emphasize the idea that the museum might act directly for the interests of the *individual human being who happens to be a child*. This is one way to demonstrate that the child's life and long survival in the world beyond the museum is of primary importance. In many ways, part of its work is not only to assist the child to lead a chosen and authentic life, but also to disencumber the child of constraints conferred by dependence on others for learning. Without subversion or disrespect to parents and teachers, the supreme communication to a child in the museum is: you are an individual learner here and you must make a learning life for yourself.

How will this happen?

- Children in museums should have sustained encounters with process, ambiguity, collaboration, and mystery, encounters leading to grounded knowledge of how thinking happens.[6]

- Children in museums should have opportunities to interpret open questions about the meanings of evidence. They need to understand that no interpretive vision of the world is perfect, no value is absolute, no view is necessarily more accurate than others.

- Every child requires time alone to choose and linger, in private. To deny this is to deny the essential nature of the institution.[7]

- Recognizing that the most powerful truths are not those given to us, nor even those we have discovered whole, but those we have crafted for ourselves out of diverse elements over time, children in museums should have opportunities to construct knowledge, rather than receive it.[8]

- Children should come to understand that the museum, both in and behind its public domains, is a system and a structure of knowledge, and that it can be a lifelong resource for the crafting of personal truths.

Libraries have mastered this concept of helping, but it is often remote in other cultural institutions. Museums must learn how to assist users. Assisted performance defines what a child can do with help, with the support of the museum staff and its communal environment. Tharp and Gallimore, in a book wonderfully titled *Rousing Minds to Life*[9] (the phrase is Vygotsky's), offer specific means for assisting classroom performance in the "proximal zone of development," Vygotsky's term for the learner's capacity to learn through specific assistance. Three of these forms of helping seem likely to occur usefully in museums: modeling, questioning, and cognitive structuring.

Modeling offers advanced exemplary behaviors to museum users in order to influence their subsequent independent performances. Among these offered behaviors or critical stances are specific ways to examine or compare objects; analogous mental processes, potentially transferable to similar objects or experiences; advanced language that expands the child's vocabulary; or key strategies that may be replicable in other settings, with other topics or objects in mind.

Questioning suggests a possible heuristic, or set of general questions, for the uncovering of a situation's hidden characteristics. The questions may offer a framework, redirect attention, evoke a memory, assess progress, or induce an alternative perspective that helps a learner to frame a problem anew and arrive at a new level of comprehension.

Every object and every concept deserves a good set of questions.

Cognitive structuring is the most complex way of assisting performance, yet it is the one most adaptable to the situation of the museum. Tharp and Gallimore write: "'Cognitive structuring' refers to the provision of a structure for thinking and acting. It may be a structure for beliefs, for mental operations, or for understanding. It is an organizing structure that evaluates, groups, and sequences perception, memory, and action. In science, it is theory; in religion it is theology; in games, it is rules."[10]

Structures may offer the learner appropriate sets of terms or operations, known relationships among physical properties, the nature of tools used to generate specific knowledge, observable qualities, or relationships that define or classify objects. "Various kinds of cognitive structures can be provided. They can be grand: worldviews, philosophies, ethical systems, scientific theories, and religious theologies. Or they can be as modest as giving a name to a thing."[11]

We need to remember that children are typically led to the museum's situations for learning by more powerful others, and are rarely given what they need to lead *themselves* into knowledge. Even though children are told about the future constantly, they are rarely given the museum or the library as lifelong instruments or resources. When given an appropriate introduction to its structures and tentative ways to think about objects, the young museum user has the initial grounding for conversations, a basis for generalizing from thing to thing, possible explanations for observed phenomena, and a way to operate in the setting. When we are helped with our first steps, or offered a recipe, or given a taxonomy or a framework, we are given a chance to build a private cognitive life.

From these structures, freely given by the institution, a learner can move gradually toward the performance of individually crafted meanings, naming for herself or himself the invisible qualities of objects, finding for himself or herself a language to communicate interior experiences, and inventing new connective structures as needed when experience requires. In this way, the museum can give children the opportunity to take charge of their own becoming, and so rouse their minds for a lifetime of crafting their own separate truths.

There is, for all of us, a time for breaking through childhood and taking up the building of a responsible learner's life. What are the influences intervening between the child and individual experiences, the influences that must be broken through? There are many, and they are often valuable elements of the child's life: the school, the family, the peer group, and other situations where membership and caring are central. When teaching and parenting are wise, they will prepare a child for the processes of becoming both responsible and adventurous. But some school and even familial enterprises specialize in keeping the child away from an individualized self.

Here I find myself drawn to talk not about childhood, exactly, but about early selfhood and the need to live life as a perpetual inquiry. I think of the child learner in the museum as a human life in progress, ready to experiment with an emerging life outside the class, group, or family. Gently but clearly, the museum can help the child become aware of the idea of cognitive growth as a lifetime journey, irrespective of schooling.

Taking charge of one's own becoming is the continuing problem of one life, for child and adult, so I will conclude by listing the kinds of skills that will help children to consider the possibilities of their own becoming. For me, these are *pursuit skills*, the things we need to know if we are to arrive at our own crafted truths:

- how to observe physical and social life while taking part in it

- how to recognize someone or something worthy of one's attention and caring and how to become interested in that life or object

- how to keep track of thoughts and communicate them through writing, if only to ourselves

- how to expand language as a tool, using its logic and power to name and order the environment

- how to go beyond the information given by asking good questions and by turning to others for help

- how to think critically and make judgments of value

- how to overcome distances in thought and experience

And I describe the following as *survival skills*, the ways we have to preserve the life we lead, and its possibilities for becoming strong. In order to survive as thinkers and learners, we need to know

- how to recognize what's worthless, harmful, or dangerous in the long run

- how to be a fearless individual in the presence of human differences—differences in values, behaviors, and ideas

- how to be a fearless individual alone

- how to read and interpret signs of need in one's own life

- how to change when necessary, and make new choices, in order to find alternate dreams and possibilities

These skills of pursuit and survival involve learning what to trust about oneself and others and how to recognize that one is always stronger than one thinks.

The potential values of the museum for children lie in its powers to advance their becoming, to enhance their understanding of capability, and to transform their perspectives on themselves and the contexts they occupy. Some years ago, researchers listed the common "gateways to the distant" that a learner encounters in everyday experience: satellite transmission, print and electronic media, long-distance communication devices, airports, and other transportation terminals.[12] These are phenomena that allow the learner to conceive of the distant, to exchange messages over distances, to understand routes and passages to other places—and in this way to ground and define the possibilities of communication between lives in time and space. Now there are so many more of these gateways at hand. They allow a child to conceive of the distant, to exchange messages, and to grasp more fully the extent of the living world.

In exactly the same terms, cultural institutions may be envisioned and constructed as gateways to the distant, places where we may see evidence of Vygotsky's idea that human beings "grow into the intellectual life of those around them."[13] Questions of art, science, social history, and human creativity offer continuing access to permanent, inviting human unknowns, the true continuities of cognitive life. Our open, continuous questions imply the sense that Jerome Bruner says must characterize human intuition: the "sense of incompleteness, the feeling that there is something more to be done."[14] It seems to me that we want learners to experience this feeling as a form of welcome, rather than intimidation or imposition.

The future museum should introduce the child to a place in the interwoven systems of experience, then the museum should assist the child "to go further," in Bruner's words, without hesitation, toward new encounters with incompleteness.

Mihaly Csikszentmihalyi writes about the welcome complexity of engagement with the world.

> It is by becoming increasingly complex that the self might be said to grow. Complexity is the result of two broad psychological processes: *differentiation* and *integration*. Differentiation implies a movement toward uniqueness, toward separating oneself from others. Integration refers to its opposite: a union with other people, with ideas and entities beyond the self.[15]

Our great cultural institutions inspire us because they are complex, offering more strands and permutations than any one mind can weave in its lifetime. And this is why museums, if their complexity is cultivated, can become ideal cognitive environments, devoted to transferring to their users a lifelong responsibility for their own becoming in a rich civilization. Great cultural institutions are able to assist youth to think in ways that open and expand the immediate experience, while creating strengths of critical thought that will last into the distance.

We encounter learning in a place where human beings complete the presence of memories, objects, texts, ideas, concepts, dreams, and possibilities—things of no meaning without a person standing in their grasp. Always, our task remains to go beyond where we are, without hesitation or fear, toward new encounters with the distant, the incomplete, and the unknown.

It seems to me that what often happens in childhood—in schools but also in families and too often in museums as well— is that we are led to stand at a window or a video screen and told to look (and then told what we are looking at), when what we need is to be taken to a river, right up to the water's edge, and taught how to move fearlessly into the stream, even though we may be swept away for a while. That is one risk of learning. And, as in the experience of swimming the river, the experience of museums depends on more than knowledge to make the difference in our survival. We want strength, and will, and an ability to see ahead. The experience of museum thinking (like the experience of swimming) is one we cannot allow someone else to have for us and then tell us about. It is crafted, practiced, and demanding, as the fabrication of any authentic artifact must be; and it is true to us, because it is our own.

Notes

This essay was based on a talk originally delivered at the Children's Museum of Indianapolis, "Thinking for the Future Museum," on April 14, 1993.

1. See Ellen J. Langer, *Mindfulness* (Reading, Mass.: Addison-Wesley, 1989); and *The Power of Mindful Learning* (Reading, Mass.: Perseus Books, 1997).

2. Frank Smith, *To Think* (New York: Teachers College Press, 1990), 95.

3. John W. Gardner, *No Easy Victories* (New York: Harper & Row, 1967), 32.

4. Smith, *To Think*, 96.

5. Jules Henry, "Vulnerability in Education," in *Jules Henry on Education* (New York: Vintage, 1972), 24.

6. A model for such encounters (in Matthew Lipman, *Thinking in Education* [New York: Cambridge University Press, 1991], 13–14) assumes no single way to think; an array of disciplines, processes, and perspectives leads discovery forward. Any assistance from another person is given in speculative, rather than in didactic or authoritative ways; the teacher admits to having questions and making errors, natural processes when working openly on problems of knowledge. In such communities of inquiry, it is expected that thought and reflection will occur—typically in the form of dialogue and interaction with others—and that these will increase reason, judgment, and strategic insight. When the museum creates situations for these qualities to emerge, it advances itself as a setting for the continuous pursuit of unanswered questions over the lifespan.

7. Even temporary freedom from a group permits the learner to experience some of the conditions that Jerome Bruner (in *The Relevance of Education*, ed. Anita Gil [New York: W. W. Norton, 1971], 84) says are required for the development of intuitive thinking: making an active commitment to the experience, self-discovery "in the field," assumption of self-confidence and possibility. Under these conditions, the child can experience the private and nonverbal encounters immediately promised to adult museum users. Working within the museum as a structure under relatively loose guidance, a child can establish processes and connections independent of a teacher or larger group.

8. With these crafted truths in mind, I suggest that the following are initial museum construction skills:

- Knowing how to ask fundamental, observation-based questions about objects and their contexts; then using these questions to organize additional observations and more complex questions.

- Participating in the active processes of knowing: documenting observations, engaging in collaborative dialogues with other museum users, critically comparing related works.

- Managing multiple strands of experience: observations, readings, exploring expert advice, and from the gathered information, synthesizing, extrapolating, interpreting, and recombining available knowledge.

- Developing expertise in the discourse surrounding objects, including the use of an appropriate museum heuristic.

- Reflecting about museum learning while away from the museum; planning steps to take on subsequent museum days.

9. Roland G. Tharp and Ronald Gallimore, *Rousing Minds to Life: Teaching, Learning and Schooling in Social Context* (New York: Cambridge University Press, 1988), 30.

10. Tharp and Gallimore, *Rousing Minds to Life*, 63.

11. Tharp and Gallimore, *Rousing Minds to Life*, 65.

12. S. H. White and A. W. Siegel, "Cognitive Development in Time and Space," in *Everyday Cognition: Its Development in Social Context*, ed. Barbara Rogoff and Jean Lave (Cambridge, Mass.: Harvard University Press, 1984), 261.

13. Lev S. Vygotsky, *Mind in Society*, ed. Michael Cole, et al. (Cambridge, Mass.: Harvard University Press, 1978), 88.

14. Jerome S. Bruner, *The Relevance of Education*, ed. Anita Gil, (New York: W. W. Norton, 1971), 86.

15. Mihaly Csikszentmihalyi, *Flow: The Psychology of Optimal Experience* (New York: Harper & Row, 1990), 41.

9

The Promise of
Cultural Institutions

Most experiences are unsayable; they happen in a
space that no word has ever entered.[1]

—Rilke

A Journey We Are on

In the autumn of 2001, the promise of cultural institutions begins
with a poem, written around forty years ago by Edward Field.[2]

A Journey

When he got up that morning everything was different:
He enjoyed the bright spring day
But he did not realize it exactly, he just enjoyed it.

And walking down the street to the railroad station
Past magnolia trees with dying flowers like old socks
It was a long time since he had breathed so simply.

Tears filled his eyes and it felt good
But he held them back
Because men didn't walk around crying in that town.

And waiting on the platform at the station
The fear came over him of something terrible about to happen:
The train was late and he recited the alphabet to keep hold.

And in its time it came screeching in
And as it went on making its usual stops,
People coming and going, telephone poles passing,

He hid his head behind a newspaper
No longer able to hold back the sobs, and willed his eyes
To follow the rational weavings of the seat fabric.

He didn't do anything violent as he had imagined.
He cried for a long time, but when he finally quieted down
A place in him that had been closed like a fist was open,

And at the end of the ride he stood up and got off that train:
And through the streets and in all the places he lived in later on
He walked, himself at last, a man among men,
With such radiance that everyone looked up and wondered.

Even after a few months in our new journey there are things we know. This place we are in is new, but somehow it is not new; it is unknown, and vast, yet still imminent and personal to us. Our parents and grandparents knew what we can behold and still live, and now so do we. We also know by now that art can counter chaos; that memory, history, and stories can embolden us when we are in the embrace of uncertainty, and help us to fathom and survive it. In the worst moments, we see ourselves, able to endure unimaginable losses. Fear weaves new strands into our fabric—but we are, mostly, unafraid.

We are unafraid because we know how to witness and to tell, how to turn toward others, and how to praise. We know how we have no choice other than to think, when our minds are in unbearable motion. We know that we are able to continue when dire knowledge comes to us unbidden, but we do not know how. What we had not seen, we saw. What we did not know, we know now. This knowing has become our journey, and now, our heroes have become the everyday rescuers of those we have lost.

In our own lives, heroism means to feel and to believe in learning and self-renewal, and growing stronger by what we experience.

He cried for a long time, but when he finally quieted down
A place in him that had been closed like a fist was open.

There are things, still, that we do not yet know and must understand. What do we want to have happen next in America's lives? In America's minds? What will our touchstones of memory be; how shall we find and keep them safe? What stories do we need to tell? What voices to hear? What lives to live? How shall we understand the configuring themes that have brought us into our third century of memory and culture, and have given us our diverse American selves over time? Of these themes, how shall we encourage our communities to speak, how shall we give words to their speechless flow?

We can never ask too many questions now. How shall we construct encounters with the self that are not selfish, encounters with knowledge independent of education, encounters with mysteries that do not evoke fear, encounters with unknowns that do not inspire anxiety?

What worlds do we wish to have open to us now, like a fist that has been closed in our hearts? What new knowledge do we require to understand human differences?

How do we find confident, fearless experiences that make an open mind possible, transforming experiences we rush to tell to those we love?

What do we need—what do we require—out of other minds than ours? What parts of their personal knowledge do we wish to evoke as a bridge to our own?

How do we help move our lives toward integrity and not despair, toward continuity, coherence, and balance? How shall we embrace our challenges and lessons, our errors, and failures? What must we learn about crafting the authentic and the true out of the evidence we have been given?

Our questions are the only ways we have of leading ourselves forward—our only ways to see a common possibility in the promise of cultural institutions. We are not at a loss; we have a mutual horizon in what we do. We share it with our companions; we are grounded in each other and we can reach toward each other. We are grounded, too, in communities of trust; by what we do, we can assist our people to reach toward something, and toward each other, out of trust and hope.

This is the idea that has been moving me forward for the second half of my life: all cultural institutions, all public voices, all structures of common memory, all situations constructed for the crafting of truth by ordinary people—all share one living genius. They are about the human thing, the being a human being, the living a life that wants, that abrades itself with questions and heals itself by learning.

A Life Unfolding

The great cultural institution is formative and collaborative. It assists the construction of personal knowledge in handmade lives. It tends to illuminate the unanticipated possibilities of knowing and feeling latent in one life. It inspires and extends the unpredictable reaches of personal knowledge and insight. It offers its users an array of guiding maps, lived lives, and lived experiences. These maps evolve with the learner over time; they mix design and hope with accident and wonder. They invite the learner in and lead the learner on.

The formative cultural institution will capture and hold dimensions of the culture at hand, and bring close images and evidences of cultures at a distance. It will address the individual life when it is most in need of renewal. It will enable individuals to renegotiate (alone or with others) their understandings of their own cultures and to recover the possibilities of discovering new truths about themselves and other persons. This institution offers new insight as the contexts, constraints, and evidences of human lives change.

We might think of cultural institutions as public laboratories for immersion in the evolving human story, its energies, processes, and interrelationships; they are the structures we have dedicated to the finding of what one person needs most to know or experience and needs most to understand.

The great institution will invite the inquirer to express personal longings in the forms of questions. It will offer sanctuary, structure, and advocacy; it will promote the individual's self-transformation. It will prepare the learner for living a life that will never be the same afterward.

Against invasive chaos, as we now know, the intelligent evolution of an individual human being requires the cognitive management of informing experiences. Intuition and logic combine in artful order: we begin, we improvise, we arrive at our few moments of clarity. For each of us, this is the challenge of living an informed life; and it is the challenge of every constructive cultural institution. We know the great institution as our partner. Mutually engaged systems, the institution and its users, can come to see a future in each other, under conditions of trust. Much depends—*everything* depends, for us, now—on trust. The community in forward motion depends on museums, libraries, public broadcasting, and other settings, because informed community policy depends on public literacy and interpretive competency, functions that take form and have meaning in human and civic processes.

Policies and community decisions will be fair and authentic when they are informed by an understanding of differences—different pasts, different paths, different ways of understanding the future—and an understanding that these differences are great, from person to person to person. The civic space in forward motion depends on its information, its records and observations, its insights and diaries, its precedents, comparisons, conversations, and stories, all taking form and meaning in literate relationships. Because we build minds with language, we are not isolated and we are not lost from each other. And because we can speak together, we can act together for the commonweal.

And yet, here in our cultural spaces, in museums and libraries, here the learner, the solitary person, the individual persists. The art of the informing institution lies in the design of structures and practices that lead to reflection and nurture change, one mind at a time. The great institution thinks with, of, and for the lives of others; and almost heroically, it is always prepared to rescue its users, always ready to connect life to life.

An individual holds in memory a mix of knowns and unknowns, experiences and imaginings, memories finished and unfinished, inquiries finished and unfinished. These fold in on each other, and then open and fold outward toward new experiences every day. An informing institution envisions the place that enveloping knowledge holds in a human life as it goes forward. As a place for human change, the institution illuminates how different an unreflective, uninformed life is from a life unfolding.

If we are to be learners, we know that our understanding is a thread, our experience the fabric, and the mind a needle. We do our best work at the edges of the fabric, where threads are loose and strands go off to something elsewhere. Our place of learning is at the edge of the fabric. In order to learn, we must go beyond what we already know, constructing for ourselves a temporary design of risk and possibility in hope of a tenuous insight. The more we have understood about the patterns of the whole fabric, the less fragile our fresh handwork at its edges.

The world in our minds is layered and multidisciplinary, the vital imaginative realm of a human thinking. Every time we need, or are afraid, we stand at the edge of disorganization and entropy, and we restore our energy only when we import new information. It is part of our nature to seek such challenges, to make ourselves uneasy in order to *become* our stronger selves in the world. We require themes and variations in knowing. We need uncertainties, confirmations, and refutations. We seek examples, then we seek challenges to them. We are always considering multiple acceptable possibilities; we are always looking for alternatives, tensions, and trouble.

"Alternatives, tensions, and trouble"—this is what cultural institutions exist to do, to bring to mind. Trouble—in the right place, form, and measure—can be a memorable and useful gift. If we are asked, "What is the problem cultural institutions address?", we might answer, "They trouble us, and so assist us in becoming who and what we are meant to be."

For example, speaking personally, I have come to respect perplexity, mystery, and reverence in Houston at the de Menil collections of Cornell, Twombly, and Rothko; and again among the Cornell boxes at the Art Institute of Chicago; and again in the presence of a Cycladic figure, just last week at the North Carolina Museum of Art. There, too, in Raleigh, when I saw a video by Bill Viola—"The Quintet of Remembrance"—I also revisited privately, in memory, a Breughel I had first seen in New York twenty years ago. Again, when I saw a painting by Bartolome Esteban Murillo of "The Blessed Giles [levitating in ecstasy] before Pope Gregory IX," completed three hundred years before my birth, I thought of Gabriel García Márquez's *One Hundred Years of Solitude*, a work I had read in 1975.

At Yellowstone, I remembered the pines from painted backgrounds at the American Museum of Natural History; I first saw them fifty years ago.

I have learned how to aspire to a life of informed depth and compassion at the Museum of Jewish Heritage in New York, and I thought of it, so ironically bathed in ashes on September 11, 2001. I am able to hear the extraordinary voices of the American South on the main street of my town, on National Public Radio, at my own university's oral history collections, and I hear them when I recall seeing the astonishing collection of American lynching photographs, gathered under the title "Without Sanctuary." Then I think of the Museum of Jewish Heritage again.

I have observed the power of literacy among families and books at the Children's Museum of Indianapolis and in the public libraries of Providence, Rhode Island, where (through the Rhode Island School of Design Museum) artists come to be with communities and work as magicians and tricksters do, transforming things, so they speak of a different realm of life, below the surfaces of things.

Borrowing Rilke's words to a young poet about the transforming qualities of deep feelings, I suggest that cultural institutions offer us "the moments when something new has entered us, something unknown; our feelings grow mute in shy embarrassment, everything in us withdraws, a silence arises, and the new experience, which no one knows, stands in the midst of it all and says nothing."[3]

And yet, of course, such moments can say everything we need to hear. What our culture withholds, our cultural institutions must give: order and form to feelings, illuminations to darkness, logics and processes to questions, rescue from the mindless undertow. "That which is not in stone," writes Eugene Guillevic, "not in the wall of stones and earth, / not even in trees, / that which forever trembles a little, / must, then, be in us."[4]

Of human beings among cultural institutions, we might say, we are not only the authors of the vision that moves us forward; we are in it as we dream it. Of ourselves among cultural institutions, we may say that we are drawn to be here and drawn to learn here as everyone is, by the enchantments of mind, passion, and desire.

The promise of cultural institutions is founded on mutual human horizons.

- We inhabit our unknowns and our unknowns inhabit us; we lead lives that carry a host of unfinished issues and questions. They are not lost causes to us: we work on them, think about them, every day. We work on them in grocery lines, bookstores, airports, magazine shops, and at family gatherings and religious ceremonies, while jogging, biking, and showering. We try to respond consciously to these unfinished parts of ourselves whenever we are in the presence of information, help, and useful evidence.

- Museums, libraries, and public broadcasting—and zoological gardens, botanical gardens, historic houses and restorations, and national parks—although an array of separate voices, offer complementary intellectual structures to learners. Identical unknowns, questions, and heuristics can be engaged in each setting. Encountered alone, however, neither information nor objects can fully satisfy many inquiries. Learners need open opportunities, where evidence and context can be encountered in depth, in dialogue with companions and mentors. Learners can learn only from other learners.

- Our institutions consequently share an urgent responsibility to construct situations where good thinking and opportunities for learning occur. Users reach toward something they are looking for but may be unable to describe, something they need but may be unable to understand, something that may transform them profoundly, but in ways they will not even notice. We exist to name, map, and observe the unknown, and it is a purpose we share with every other person.

• And there is the pointed truth of our situation: learning is always the process of being moved by invisible actions, led by hands whose touch we feel but whose bodies we cannot see.

What institutions would we construct and what messages would we give if we knew that every person living carries the seed of an insight so profound that, if nurtured, it might later come to mind every subsequent day of our lives? What if we knew that every person in our communities was almost imperceptibly engaged in fulfilling, over time, the early promise of some childhood fascination? What would our task be if we knew that people learn because they are attuned to their own unique themes or motifs, repeated and deepened with variations like music over the entire span of life?

Incompleteness

How are we to construct our cultural institutions to matter in the lived experiences of our users? The most formative learning, the kind that will lead a person toward a grounded and continuous life, is learning that recognizes its own incompleteness. Its value must be proven, not in the abstract, but in the consequences and fulfillments of human lives and relationships.

If you are an educator, you know that to assist other learners you will encounter yourself repeatedly. You will remove falsity, arrogance, and pretension. You must rescue yourself first. Whatever teaching transforms others, will also transform you. The future of the learner in the new century is the professional future as well: challenged, fragmentary, fluid, complex. Given the narrow constraints of an education that embraces reductive testing and evaluation, I think it is a world where schooling will matter less and less to the processes of becoming a human being, and perhaps one day it will mean not much at all.

Does anyone in schools say to the learner, young or old, "My job is to assure that you do not miss the best possible life you were meant to live?" This is what we must say, I think. Perhaps, I think, a reductive, test-centered education will not help much to construct curious, great minds. And so it is now ours to do, as part of our promise.

It is reasonable to believe that the future is about managing information. But this future is also about managing other things we cannot see: tension, ambiguity, and reflection. We may worry about such things, but they are exactly the qualities that lead to artistry, design, and insight in living one life. It is my habit to invite them—tension, ambiguity, and reflection—into my life and the lives of my students, so they are always present to us, shaping us as we read and experience our work.

If they are to be mindful of their users, professionals in cultural settings ought to feel invited by learning lives of their own, practice the critical thinking that leads to new levels of service, diagnose communities and learners in change, and learn to suspend judgment in the presence of difficult issues. A practice of artistry, design, and insight will follow from any of these things:

- an awareness of the other, and the challenges of other lives

- knowledge of the logics, tools, and structures that organize information and give it value for others

- skill in the observation of situations, circumstances, and contexts where other people stand in need of knowledge

- an understanding of the tensions of practice and service as problems to be addressed anew every day

- a daily weaving and reweaving of the possibilities for learning

- an unhesitatingly active stance, the stance of a champion for the user

- and a willingness to ask in every moment of planning and reflecting: How does this rescue the learner?

Artistry in practice asks of us these things: attention to one's own intellectual life; the interpretation of possibilities for another human being; and the making of insightful, even graceful, connections among minds, tasks and information.

Enemies of Learning

There are enemies of learning, but I encourage you to be fearless in your encounters with them because you stand in a rich landscape of possibility and integrity. When we consider and address the individual *as a learner,* we are considering the person in the most human way possible, the essential way that best characterizes the human place in the cycles of life on earth. When you assist a learner to craft a personal observation, you are expressing the profoundest respect for the human being as the author of his or her own experiences. The moment of insight and exquisite surprise, the moment of recognition and consolation, the deeply embedded and yet subtly moving thing within—are treasures and privileges to express or witness.

There are countless hopeful and inspiring ideas to take into this century, allowing them to open in our work.

- the most important idea is the comprehension of a human lifespan and the continuous renewal of awareness through learning over its journey

- the idea that over time we craft or construct and do not passively receive what we come to know as true

- the idea that we can find energy in the possibilities of a debated and flawed past, where diversities, inequities, myths, and misuses of history are part of what we are required to interpret today

- the idea that we should emphasize the power of the authentic, always made clearer by the presence of the imitative, the sham, the phony, and the cheap

- the idea that we should understand ourselves as central in the emerging definition of the information society and its more important successor, the growing culture of knowledge

- the idea that there is strength in the emergent idea of the cultural institution and its professionals as educators, actively transmitting the grounded experiences and cultural messages of our collections

- the idea that the possibilities of defining collaborative missions, community projects, and conversations across all collections are ours

We should be heartened, as well, because a culture of lifelong encounters with knowledge is ours. Even more deeply than our schools, museums and libraries are the primary designers of adult encounters with authentic knowledge in this culture.

So I encourage you to understand the enemies of learning.

It seems clear that humans are vulnerable to the undertow of mindlessness. At the risk of heresy, I suggest that the enemy of learning is commercial entertainment. Therefore, our promise must be first to inform and suggest; to present information and the record of inquiry accurately and in depth; to imply by our caring and demonstration the pleasure of questioning; to articulate the inviting unknowns still to be explored; to engage the user in mysteries; to avoid the curriculum of passive amusement. We ought to assure the prevalence of engagement, expression, and play in its place.

We know that human beings are in constant evolution, subject to tensions, questions, and uncertainties. So I remind you that the enemy of learning is assumption, the arrogant thinking that we know best. Therefore, the work of every cultural institution must begin by talking to the user, involving the user in tentative dialogues and conversations, or else the user will never find a future in its collections.

For the moment, it seems that human tools and processes are the captives of speed, access, and miniaturization. So I remind you that the enemy of learning is reduction. Therefore, it is part of our promise to explain depths, to explain the array of paths and the continuities each implies, and to explain and map the complexities of interdisciplinarity. Pleasure in learning, strength of commitment to learn, and the complexity of our pursuits are positively connected; they require each other. We are wise to explain that learning requires investments of time, and to introduce and practice the art of the reflective pause. Consider the possibility that cultural institutions are the permanent refuge of the slow learner in all of us.

Human beings live through and are configured by common themes, but these themes are often invisible. Our lives are continuous with other lives, but these continuities are typically unspoken. I encourage you to speak them out loud, because the enemy of learning is disconnection. Therefore, in our promise to the learner we must create connective forums. Construct alliances among people and institutions, either momentary or long lasting. Understand that in sharing stories, common experiences, and differing interpretations of memory, even through stark questions and misunderstandings, we discover a great common heritage living embedded in our narratives, experiences, and aspirations.

We may observe that human beings become encapsulated, isolated, private, even fearful and hesitant at the edges of life. I suggest that the enemy of learning is certainty. Therefore, we fulfill our promise when we create sustained situations for intellectual risk. We will be wise to live, ourselves, with the knowledge that it is more educative and inviting to be a questioner, to be a problem solver, to be puzzled for a time—even for a long time—than it is to live for the answer alone. Frank Smith writes, "Certainty stunts thought, in ourselves and others. . . . All thinking is based on 'suppose things were different.'"[5]

There is a tendency to see museums and libraries as public places where all problems have been solved, and they merely await our attention. Rather, it is important to see that they are the shops where problems are perpetually refreshed, assembled, and discovered. The strengths of our hearts and minds, as we have recently learned among our losses, are proven amid the persistence of uncertainty. Suppose things were different, indeed.

Learners need to trust themselves and their own perceptions; we all need to become people we can ourselves recognize and embrace—neither too small to have great and wonderful ideas, nor too grand to learn among others. We all need to construct meaning and knowledge on a human scale, and we need to feel authorship for it. And so, with unlimited respect and admiration for teachers—because I *am* a teacher— I suggest that the enemy of learning is instruction. Therefore, it is part of the promise of every cultural institution to create situations for self-designed experiences, experiences that confuse and challenge, experiences that follow from other experiences and lead to clarifying experiences. Experiences that allow mysteries. Experiences that respect the unknown but assist its erosion. And teachers who create moments for conversations between human beings and the continuing complexities that are their lives.

I know that we will always work in museums and libraries in an uneasy relationship with the massive authority and pervasive ubiquity of the school. This does not always permit the cultural institution to be seen in its own right, with its own lessons for learners.

As a teacher who still loves to teach teachers and to visit schools, I must always remind myself that schools tend to create somewhat dissonant mental maps for learners; as you may recall, their plans are often disciplinary, linear, and reductive. They are too often driven by testing. They tend to avoid learning through apprenticeships, through storytelling, through experimentation and reflection. They tend to be competitive when we would hope them to be more collaborative. I worry that we may have generations of students who grow old with an illiteracy of feeling, an inability to think with passion, an idea that love and mind do not connect, and that a shallow heart is a safe one.

We know that the message from a responsive, collaborative, giving experience—animated by the genius of the human being—is different for us all. I look at schoolchildren (and sometimes including my graduate students) and ask, "How will they come to be lifelong learners? How will they catch fire and recover their radiance?"

(But then my student Kelly submits a paper about "The Experience of Mind in Public Space,"[6] and writes, "I want my heart to hear what my mind comes up with. I want my mind informed by what my heart knows." In a later sentence, she writes, "When people are given the space to feel fully and react and think to their best ability, they will develop differently than when they are cut off from their emotional and thinking lives." And then, my student Catherine writes, "We place a high value . . . on learning—and yet we have an educational system that was not designed to produce learners."[7] And Christine writes, "If we are unwilling to become a vessel, we will not free ourselves to let the world fill us."[8] And Jessica, a reader, writes: "Books are an opportunity to take a chance on a different life without fear."[9] And Elizabeth: "The public space of communities is the frame of freedom."[10] And, writing on "The Place of Memory," my student Kim says,

> Living and learning in the shadow of these memories, we are given the opportunity to become more mindful in the present. . . . It takes time for me to formulate my questions and my ideas. I ruminate. Reflecting on my own patterns of behavior and needs in these cultural institutions, I feel that I am also more capable of imagining the needs of others and noticing the messages in their behavior.[11]

As always, radiance appears before me, if only I can sense it.)

If they are to overcome the lasting effects of schooling on our spirits and thoughts, our cultural institutions must demand of their users great strength of mind; otherwise they will never see clearly the traces of an inspired hand. We do not invite learners to be bold and constructive often enough. We do not often enough recognize that what happens in cultural institutions happens in *lives*, and that it does not happen only once; it happens in the remembering and the reimagining, in the retelling and reordering of it. Our work is to begin long, impassioned conversations between intellect and spirit, talks that we will never hear.

The Enormous Assaults of the Universe

If we are to become great learners, we all must be permeable to the lived and living experiences and words of others, feeling safe enough in our own lives to encounter new questions that expand our grasp and challenge our courage. It is important to ask, "Who will be the audience for cultural institutions in the twenty-first century?," and in response, we must imagine strong men and women:

- people striving to lead lives that are not guided by accidents, inconsistencies, irrationality, or fear

- people daring to see themselves in the largest contexts— contexts at least larger than their own lives and families—in communities, societies, and nations

- people challenged to overcome the discomforts of a world where significant, pervasive ambiguities are present, and who are willing to talk about ambiguity and its consequences for action and belief in a living community

- people who assume nothing other than what they have experienced and understood, who are willing to take the time and energy to craft and reflect, and who are willing to question and confirm the testimony of others

As it ever has been, the promise of cultural institutions is greatest for users with unfinished issues in their lives—the steady, great, illuminating questions that may come early to us and become neither less complex nor more easily resolved as our lives go forward. The guiding metaphor for the cultural institution is the building of useful bridges for these others, and the transmission of pertinent building codes to the learners who will carry out this construction: the framing and shoring, and the first tentative step to test its strength.

Every cultural institution I have ever seen has virtual or actual *systems* in place that could lead the user on to ask new questions about experience; most of these systems are completely invisible to the user; some are arrogant, complex, and privileged. A heuristic— a small set of fundamental questions reflecting the record of human traces and the use of the institution as a passage to knowledge—might help the processes of inquiry. The heuristic ought to respond to the commitments and values inherent in the mission of the institution; the heuristic is a way to reinterpret and renegotiate the contractual quality of that ethos each day, in the presence of nothing that, from day to day, is ever the same.[12] As I often say in both museums and libraries: We must rescue the user.

Of every cultural institution we might say that its *reason for being* remains unfulfilled until it is completed by the expanding presence of an individual mind, aware of both the mystery and passion in its stories and the logic and possibility of knowledge surrounding them. The person at your threshold has a lifetime of brilliant choices to make, under an impossible constraint—the finitude of all human things.

I have suggested that the voice of the great institution must also be *incendiary* and *challenging*, inspiring to learners and thinkers, inviting them to a setting where mindfulness cannot be abjured. Once we have entered, we must think our way out. The institution's role is to lead by defining this voice. There is no purposeful becoming for anyone without a leading vision, but this vision cannot be transferred easily to another mind. It is inherent in the way we give ourselves and our help.

This is the final theme to consider in mapping the future: the way we encourage self-renewal, remembering and overcoming. This last element of our promise is also the first: to be generous and kind in reaching toward the original lives of other people, in order to give them the gift of a new, provocative, and increasingly pertinent idea. This is that generative part of ourselves that must now open like the fist within. It is in the essential nature of our promise to invite and explore the unspoken possibilities of human transformation, and to be unafraid as we do so.

There is only one way to assure that the possibilities of collaboration, mutual engagement, and service for the common-weal will be explored in this fearless way, and that is to be daring and open and generous when we speak together. *Daring, open,* and *generous* ought to be our guiding words for this century, and our gifts to learners in it.

The twenty-first century challenges us to transfer to the learner the invitation to encounter the great continuing unknowns of human experience, and to find them reflected in the personal continuing unknowns of one single life. Our promise is met when we understand and serve people who are crafting themselves and their truths, reaching far by using the information, observations, images, and voices we have made possible for them to use, out of our deepest respect for their integrity and courage.

Preparing to think and write of such things, I rediscovered these words of James Agee, from *Let Us Now Praise Famous Men*:

> All that each person is, and experiences, and shall never experience, in body and mind, all these things are differing expressions of himself and of one root, and are identical: and not one of these things nor one of these persons is ever quite to be duplicated, nor replaced, nor has it ever quite had precedent: but each is a new and incommunicably tender life, wounded in every breath and almost as hardly killed as easily wounded: sustaining, for a while, without defense, the enormous assaults of the universe.[13]

It is our common trust to serve and assist the American journey, fearless in this transformed century. We are perhaps at the edge of understanding that our institutions, like all of our culture, are about the energies of dream, and courage, solace and renewal. And at that edge, perhaps we can assist others (and ourselves) to understand that what we want most deeply to know as true, we must craft for ourselves. We, in the autumn of the year 2001, are at an edge of time when we have no choice except to reflect and change, a time when, in Adrienne Rich's words, "the pain of living becomes more than you can explain by your previous interpretations of the world."[14]

Notes

Presented as the keynote address for the conference on the 21st Century Learner, Institute for Museum and Library Services, Washington, D.C., November 7, 2001. I am grateful for the comments of my colleagues Claudia Gollop, Brian Sturm, Theresa Church, and Meredith Evans on an early draft of this paper.

1. Rainer Maria Rilke, *Letters to a Young Poet*, trans. Stephen Mitchell (New York: Vintage, 1986), 4.

2. Edward Field, "A Journey," in *Counting Myself Lucky: Selected Poems 1963–1992* (Santa Rosa, Calif.: Black Sparrow Press, 1992), 185.

3. Rilke, *Letters to a Young Poet*, 83.

4. Eugene Guillevic, "Where?," in *Selected Poems*, trans. Denise Levertov (New York: New Directions, 1969), 45.

5. Frank Smith, *To Think* (New York: Teachers College Press, 1990), 129.

6. Kelly Overton, "The Experience of Mind in Public Space," unpublished course paper (School of Information and Library Science, University of North Carolina at Chapel Hill, October 2001).

7. Catherine Signorile, Untitled, unpublished course paper (School of Information and Library Science, University of North Carolina at Chapel Hill, October 2001).

8. Christine Stachowicz, "Memory, Reflective Living, and Lifelong Learning: A Personal Essay," unpublished course paper (School of Information and Library Science, University of North Carolina at Chapel Hill, October 2001).

9. Jessica Kilfoil, "Final Thoughts," unpublished course paper (School of Information and Library Science, University of North Carolina at Chapel Hill, November 2001).

10. Elizabeth Johnson, Untitled, unpublished course paper (School of Information and Library Science, University of North Carolina at Chapel Hill, November 2001).

11. Kim Duckett, "Final Reflections," unpublished course paper (School of Information and Library Science, University of North Carolina at Chapel Hill, November 2000).

12. In some settings, notes on the history, science, and art news of the day, as found in *The New York Times,* might help us all to understand our tensions, our vulnerabilities, and our genius.

13. James Agee, *Let Us Now Praise Famous Men* (Boston: Houghton Mifflin, 1960).

14. Adrienne Rich, *What Is Found There* (New York: W. W. Norton, 1993), 147.

10

Ten Lessons and One Rule

Ten Lessons and One Rule

Lesson One	Learners learn from learners.
Lesson Two	Truth is crafted over time, by individuals working alone, open to the insights of others.
Lesson Three	Museums and libraries are maps and forums for their cultures. They are places for discovering edges and questioning ourselves.
Lesson Four	A configuration of stories and voices brings a community into place.
Lesson Five	At every moment, our lives carry unfinished issues. At every moment, we strive to craft the truths that will fulfill them.
Lesson Six	A great learner is a human artifact, the fabric of generous experiences and convivial relationships.
Lesson Seven	Education constructs and hones individual integrity.

Lesson Eight	An educator reopens and restores the possibilities of reflection.
Lesson Nine	A learner's process is an art; its tensions derive from and generate energy and change.
Lesson Ten	These are some of the enemies of learning: arrogance, reduction, discontinuity, entertainment, fear, and didacticism. The first two are the worst.
One Rule	Rescue the user. Every learner needs an advocate, needs to hear and trust a nearby voice.

Appendix A: Selected Readings

My work in this book will be completed when the reader looks elsewhere, among the authors below and their bibliographies, for fresher and more renewing insights. These writers and their works deserve continuous attention and discussion in cultural settings, particularly when we strive to understand the clearly public and intensely private encounters with knowledge that typify museums and libraries. Several of the books listed here are ideal selections for reading groups among professionals or preparatory readings for long-range planning.

The books by Bruner, Csikszentmihalyi, Greene, and Smith, for example, might help institutions address fundamental questions of identity and purpose. Cremin, Dewey, both Gardners, and Illich will lead to useful reflections on the nature of ideal institutions for learning. Lave and Wenger, Rogoff, and Vygotsky help us think about situations for learning in specific ways. Schön inspires practice; John-Steiner illuminates creative thinking.

Of course, new works continue to emerge. Consequently, an even larger shelf of such writers is essential. There can be no single source, reference work,[1] or textbook that will fully address the human desire for insight, the educative challenges of thought and pursuit, or the motives that bring learners to institutions. Like the users of cultural institutions, our task as readers is to make connections, fill gaps, and entertain possibilities. And so, for each one of these titles, two or three others might be added. An invitation to wide further reading is likely to follow from any book listed here.

As the essay citations make clear to the reader, most of these authors have been present voices in my thinking for many years (Often I fear they are too present, then I fear they are never present enough.), and they will always remain important in my approach to the promise of cultural institutions. As I continue to read on in other works, I am deeply grateful to have been the reader of these books first, and I will always be an admirer of the intelligence, grace, and courage they contain. In the slight annotations offered here, I have sought to place each work and its writer in a brief context, especially as they have had meaning for me over time. Page numbers for quoted passages are in parentheses and additional titles are cited in brackets. Please, reader, read on.

Jerome Bruner. *Actual Minds, Possible Worlds*. Cambridge, Mass.: Harvard University Press, 1986.

This book opens eyes and makes profound connections among the formative thinkers about learning in the twentieth century; Jerome Bruner himself must be regarded as one of these. Here, the idea of language is the critical currency for learners; it is the principal tool for negotiating the meaning of concepts. Bruner articulates these abstractions with great power and value.

> Once one takes the view that a culture itself comprises an ambiguous text that is constantly in need of interpretation by those who participate in it, then the constitutive role of language in creating social reality becomes a topic of practical concern. . . . If one is arguing about social "realities" like democracy or equity or even gross national product, the reality is

not the thing, not in the head, but in the act of arguing and negotiating about the meaning of such concepts. (p. 122)

In these passages, Bruner offers a broad view of the cultural institution as a potential forum for acting and speaking, and for undertaking the process of "exploring the possible" that transforms our questions into mindful understandings of how we live.

[See also Jerome Bruner. *On Knowing: Essays for the Left Hand*. Cambridge, Mass.: Harvard University Press, 1962; *Acts of Meaning*. Cambridge, Mass.: Harvard University Press, 1990; *The Culture of Education*. Cambridge, Mass.: Harvard University Press, 1996; Ellen J. Langer. *Mindfulness*. Reading, Mass.: Addison-Wesley, 1989.]

Lawrence A. Cremin. *Public Education*. New York: Basic Books, 1976.

This small book offers enormous ideas. The most important of them is the concept of the "configuration of education" (p. 30), the "multiplicity of institutions that educate," often interacting and sustaining multiple "overlapping lines of support and control." Schools, religions, teams, employers, libraries, museums, volunteer organizations—all of these have specific influences on the evolving construction of one life and the emergence of an adult learning style that mediates among them.

> Individuals come to educational situations with their own temperaments, histories, and purposes, and different individuals will obviously interact with a given configuration of education in different ways and with different outcomes. . . . The result will surely be a unique interaction, the outcome of which cannot be predicted by looking at either the institution(s) or the individual in isolation. (pp. 37, 40–41)

[Also: Gordon Allport. *Becoming: Basic Considerations for a Psychology of Personality.* New Haven, Conn.: Yale University Press, 1955; Mary Catherine Bateson. *Composing a Life.* New York: Atlantic Monthly Press, 1989.]

Mihaly Csikszentmihalyi. *Flow: The Psychology of Optimal Experience.* New York: Harper & Row, 1990.

The generative idea of *flow*—referring to our most optimal experiences, moments when all our skills, energies and interests focus on a satisfactory experience, moment or event—pervades Csikszentmihalyi's important work; this volume is more summative than others. The user of cultural institutions stands perfectly within the concepts used here to define experiences of flow: her experiences involve privacy, depth of attention, intrinsic rewards, and a feeling of separation from the mundane. These are experiences of thought and engagement, freely chosen from an array of other possibilities. Csikszentmihalyi writes,

> The point is that playing with ideas is extremely exhilarating. Not only philosophy but the emergence of new scientific ideas is fueled by the enjoyment one obtains from creating a new way to describe reality. The tools that make the flow of thought possible are common property, and consist of the knowledge recorded in books available in schools and libraries. (p. 127)

And, it is easy to add, in the information available in all cultural institutions.

[Also: Mihaly Csikszentmihalyi. *Beyond Boredom and Anxiety.* San Francisco: Jossey-Bass, 1977; *Optimal Experience: Psychological Studies of Flow in Consciousness* (edited, with Isabella Selega Csikszentmihalyi). New York: Cambridge University Press, 1988; *The Art of Seeing: An Interpretation of the Aesthetic Encounter* (with Rick E. Robinson). Malibu, Calif.: J. P. Getty Museum, 1990; *The Evolving Self*. New York: Harper Collins, 1993; and the works of Vera John-Steiner.]

John Dewey. *Experience and Education*. New York: Collier Books, 1963 [1938].

The first sentence of Dewey's *Democracy and Education* is this: "The most notable distinction between living and inanimate things is that the former maintain themselves by renewal." Even when we are no more than a simple visitor—mild, passive, and receptive – in a cultural institution, we are participants in the continuously renewing educative experiences of the place. Our simple presence amid information, systems, and artifacts implies the dimensions of possibility and inquiry latent in the setting. When we actively create an experience, we are evoking what Dewey called the "means and goal of education" (p. 89). Education is resonant experience that continues to happen into the future, if the mind is awakened to its dimensions and connections among objects and other minds. Consequently, "The educator by the very nature of his work is obliged to see his present work in terms of what it accomplishes, or fails to accomplish, for a future whose objects are linked with those of the present" (p. 76). Reading Dewey helps us to understand that all human behavior can be innovative and original, and that the lessons to be taken from our observations will never be complete. "No experience lives and dies to itself," Dewey writes, "Wholly independent of desire or intent, every experience lives on in further experiences" (p. 27).

[Also: John Dewey. *Democracy and Education*. New York: The Free Press, 1966 (1916); *The Philosophy of John Dewey*. Chicago: University of Chicago Press, 1981; and the works of Maxine Greene and Jack Mezirow, listed below.]

Erik H. Erikson. *The Life Cycle Completed* (extended version, with new chapters by Joan M. Erikson). New York: W. W. Norton, 1997.

The importance of the Eriksonian "stages of life" lies as deeply embedded in language as it does in psychology; this is not surprising in a work grounded on Shakespearean metaphor. For each of the stages described from infancy to old age, Erikson identifies competing qualities and related critical tensions in the course of growth. In early childhood, for example, the individual experiences a tension between *autonomy* and *shame* or *doubt*; aided primarily by parents, the child comes to terms with the basic strength embodied as *will*. In adolescence, the tension is between *identity* and *identity confusion*, leading toward the strengths of *fidelity* and an emerging *ideology*. In adulthood, the tension is between *generativity* and *stagnation*; in old age, between *integrity* and *despair*. These terms for a life's progress are powerful because they express human qualities that emerge in an individual's social and ethical relationships as well as in his or her cognitive work. In an examined life, we can recognize the struggle to sustain hope and trust against the odds, in order to find authentic satisfaction. Erikson's stages also identify the general conditions (*generativity, integrity*) that characterize a caring and wise life. They are critical terms for cultural institutions to consider and apply as they strive to understand the contributing roles of the institution over the evolving individual lifespan.

Howard Gardner. *The Unschooled Mind: How Children Think and How Schools Should Teach*. New York: Basic Books, 1991.

To the reflective cultural institution, Gardner's work offers an inspiring range of possibilities for conceptualizing human intelligences in form and function. He has made a strong and appealing case for understanding every mind's work as a personal, original, and divergent process guided by intuitive and essential competencies. As in his earlier work, *Frames of Mind*, Gardner identifies "the flowering of several intelligences in the opening years of life," a period he says "harbors more of the secrets and power of human growth than any other comparable phase" of development (p. 82). These are powerful and resonant metaphors. In this book, Gardner links the idea of multiple intelligences to the idea of apprenticeship as an alternative approach to the constraints of classrooms. In the evocative contexts of cultural institutions, Gardner asks, "Would we not be consigning students to ruination if we enrolled them in museums instead of schools?" His answer: "I believe we would be doing precisely the opposite" (p. 202).

[Also: Howard Gardner. *Frames of Mind: The Theory of Multiple Intelligences*. New York: Basic Books, 1983; *Creating Minds*. New York: Basic Books, 1993; Howard Gruber. *Darwin on Man*. Chicago: University of Chicago Press, 1982.]

John W. Gardner. *Self-Renewal: The Individual and the Innovative Society*. New York: Harper & Row, 1964.

The idea that moves through each of Gardner's small but brilliant volumes (such as *Excellence* and *No Easy Victories*), and especially through this one, is the need for "a system or framework within which continuous innovation, renewal and rebirth can occur" (p. 5). In articulating this idea, he also describes the qualities of the individual learner most adapted to the best situations and learning environments a self-renewing culture provides. Among these characteristics is "an extraordinary capacity to find the order that underlies . . . varied experience." The truly creative person, he writes, "is not an outlaw but a lawmaker" (pp. 38–39). While Gardner's subject is the individual as an actor and thinker engaged in the process of self-transformation, every word he writes applies to societies and institutions as well.

Maxine Greene. *The Dialectic of Freedom*. New York: Teachers College Press, 1988.

This work is so rich with themes and ideas, with readings and applications to the multiple situations of lived experience, that it is an essential work for the contemplation of cultural institutions, our only public settings for multiple realizations of mind. For Greene, learners require situations where new understandings of capability and self can occur, typically in applied dialogues with others. Through others, one confirms a self.

> To recognize the role of perspective and vantage point, to recognize at the same time that there are always multiple perspectives and multiple vantage points, is to recognize that no accounting, disciplinary or otherwise, can ever be finished or complete. There is always more. There is always possibility. And this is where the space opens for the pursuit of freedom. (p. 128)

[Also: Maxine Greene. *Releasing the Imagination: Essays on Education, the Arts, and Social Change.* San Francisco: Jossey-Bass, 1995; and *Variations on a Blue Guitar: The Lincoln Center Institute Lectures on Aesthetic Education.* New York: Teachers College Press, 2001.]

Ivan Illich. *Deschooling Society.* New York: Harper & Row, 1971.

More than thirty years later, Illich's early messages in *Deschooling Society* still apply to the unfulfilled promises of museums and libraries: in his view, the principles, values, and structures of schooling are formative, pervasive, and inimical. "The pupil is . . . 'schooled' to confuse teaching with learning, grade advancement with education, a diploma with competence, and fluency with the ability to say something new" (p. 1), he writes in his initial chapter, "Why We Must Disestablish Schools." Museums and libraries, so often at the direct service of the school, are affected by the kinds of schooled minds and values brought through their doors, generation by generation. Presciently writing about "learning webs" a generation before the Internet, Illich asks the fundamental question about convivial education: "What kinds of things and people might learners want to be in contact with in order to learn?" When taken to the truly convivial environments of the museum and the library, this question can begin useful processes of revision and engagement with collections.

Vera John-Steiner. *Notebooks of the Mind: Explorations of Thinking.* Albuquerque: University of New Mexico Press, 1985.

John-Steiner's subject is the mind of the genius reflecting on itself, its workings, and the patterns of creative solving that art and science share. Using diaries, interviews, letters, and other records of process, these *Notebooks* adduce thematic commonalities of language, imagery, apprenticeship, process, emotion, and passion that appear in the lives of diversely creative individuals. John-Steiner's informants are scientists, writers, filmmakers, choreographers, painters, photographers, psychologists, mathematicians, and a vast array of past geniuses who described their thoughts. "Thinking," she asks herself,

> How shall I define it? It is a soundless dialogue, it is a search for meaning. The activity of thought contributes to and shapes all that is specifically human. In building upon past knowledge, men and women transform the known—and the culturally transmitted means of knowledge—into new discoveries and into the ever-changing forms of thought and language. (p. 210)

[Also: Vera John-Steiner. *Creative Collaborations.* New York: Oxford University Press, 2000.]

Jean Lave and Etienne Wenger. *Situated Learning: Legitimate Peripheral Participation.* New York: Cambridge University Press, 1991.

Like Barbara Rogoff's *Apprenticeship in Thinking*, Lave and Wenger's *Situated Learning* assumes that a person learns as "an integral part of generative social practice in the lived-in world" (p. 35). Human change is constant and open ended, evolving out of an individual's participation with others in a social, cultural, and structural situation. "Participation is always based on situated negotiation and renegotiation of meaning in the world. This implies that understanding and experience are in constant interaction—indeed, are mutually constitutive . . . persons, actions, and the world are implicated in all thought, speech, knowing, and learning" (pp. 51–52).

[Also: Gavriel Salomon, editor. *Distributed Cognitions: Psychological and Educational Considerations*. Cambridge, U.K.: Cambridge University Press, 1993.]

Jack Mezirow and Associates. *Learning as Transformation*. San Francisco: Jossey-Bass, 2000.

Adult education theory provides useful insights for addressing adults as learners in a lifelong process; it also assists cultural institutions to invite learners for adult experiences of self-renewal. Works by Allen Tough, Alan Knox, and originators like Cyril Houle and Malcolm Knowles deserve prominence in any bibliography devoted to learning in cultural institutions. *Learning as Transformation* begins with Mezirow's own essay, "Learning to Think Like an Adult," meaning an adult's ability to rethink the ways of seeing the world. Transformative learning is based on critically reflective questions, and on a rethinking of our assumptions and guiding values, in order to arrive at new ideas. "Imagination is central to understanding the unknown; it is the way we examine alternative interpretations of our experience by 'trying on' another's point of view. The more reflective and open we are to the perspectives of others, the richer our imagination of alternative contexts and understandings will be" (p. 20).

[Also: Jack Mezirow and Associates. *Fostering Critical Reflection in Adulthood: A Guide to Transformative and Emanicipatory Learning*. San Francisco: Jossey-Bass, 1990.]

Nel Noddings. *Caring*. Berkeley: University of California Press, 1984.

"The primary aim of every educational institution and of every educational effort must be the maintenance and enhancement of caring" (p. 172), Noddings writes, in a book that places caring at the apex of the nurturant and ethical ideals that characterize institutions of every kind. "[Caring] functions as end, means and criterion for judging suggested means. It establishes the climate, a first approximation to the range of acceptable practices, and a lens through which all practices and possible practices are examined" (p. 172). The ethic of caring is pertinent to all critical aspects of cultural engagement and social purpose: it is central to scholarship and learning, to the institutional fabric, and to the urgencies of civic life. To read Noddings is to understand not only the implications of what caring means; it is to understand the arrogance and irresponsibility of carelessness when we experience it.

[Also: Nel Noddings and Paul J. Shore. *Awakening the Inner Eye: Intuition in Education*. New York: Teachers College Press, 1984.]

Barbara Rogoff. *Apprenticeship in Thinking: Cognitive Development in Social Context*. New York: Oxford University Press, 1990.

The central idea of apprenticeship, as Rogoff describes it, can be applied directly to cultural institutions, either in the sense of individual collaborations between an experienced person and a learner, or in the sense of assisting others to think of themselves as learners as they observe and experience skills required by complex activities. Guided participation in events—where a learner gradually but systematically learns the structures and patterns of an experience—places cognitive growth directly in the context of a social, mutually shared situation. "Development is built on the transformations and rhythms intrinsic to life; what needs explanation is the direction of change and the patterns of life that organize change in specific directions" (p. 13). Tools, technologies, contexts, information, and the guiding voice of a master surround the learner, directing attention, demonstrating approaches, and trying out solutions. For a learner, learning through apprenticeship slows down the encounter with knowledge, requires a transfer of skills and perspectives between humans in the context of the learning, and encourages inventions and decisions that move the learner toward expertise.

[Also: Michael W. Coy, editor. *Apprenticeship: From Theory to Method and Back Again.* Albany: State University of New York Press, 1989; Sylvia Farnham-Diggory. *Schooling.* Cambridge, Mass.: Harvard University Press, 1990.]

Donald A. Schön. *The Reflective Practitioner: How Professionals Think in Action.* New York: Basic Books, 1983.

This highly original work about professional problem solving offers a sense of how an institution can come to understand itself, redesign its practices, and act with ideas and values in the foreground. By examining a series of practical professional situations, Schön addresses the ways an institution can transform decisions and actions for change into processes of thought and design. When an institution, for example, needs to develop a group of colleagues who approach their work as a series of moves and reflections on consequences—and come to see their practice as inquiry—this work can be an inspiration. Schön's ideas are complex but essential to this prospect, and will stimulate the conversations such transformations require.

[Also: Donald A. Schön. *Educating the Reflective Practitioner*. San Francisco: Jossey-Bass, 1987.]

Frank Smith. *To Think*. New York: Teachers College Press, 1990.

"Thought creates realities," Smith writes (p. 109). His resonant observations on the everyday concepts of thought and thinking expand and deepen our awareness and understanding of what happens when humans engage in mental acts. "The range of human thought is infinite and awesome. The realities that we are capable of entering are not accounted for by conventional theories of language, art, or perception. They reflect a fundamental propensity of the human brain to invent—and exploit—new possibilities. Thought is relentlessly creative" (p. 71).

[Also: Frank Smith. *The Book of Learning and Forgetting*. New York: Teachers College Press, 1998.]

Allen Tough. *Intentional Changes: A Fresh Approach to Helping People Change*. Chicago: Follett, 1982.

A professor of adult education at the Ontario Institute of Education, Allen Tough conducted studies leading to the landmark works, *Why Adults Learn: A Study of Tasks and Assistance During Adult Self-Teaching Projects* and *The Adult's Learning Projects: A Fresh Approach to Theory and Practice in Adult Learning*. Tough's research, devoted to defining and understanding the dynamics of adult self-directed learning, was extremely significant in defining the roles of adult educators as they assist individual learning projects to take form. *Intentional Changes* holds a treasury of practice insights for professionals in cultural institutions who recognize the pervasive presence of dedicated learners in need of focus, tools, and occasional assistance to accomplish their learning goals. Though no longer recent, Tough's work still retains its fresh sensibility. It helps us understand that libraries and museums can be agencies as well as collections, and that all institutions can be educational resources for long-term learning.

Lev S. Vygotsky. *Mind in Society: The Development of Higher Psychological Processes*, edited by Michael Cole, Vera John-Steiner, Sylvia Scribner, and Ellen Souberman. Cambridge, Mass.: Harvard University Press, 1978.

John Dewey's sentence, "Every experience is a moving force" (*Experience and Education*, p. 38), and Vygotsky's definition of the "zone of proximal development" (ZPD) in *Mind in Society* (p. 86), are perhaps the most powerful educational concepts ever articulated for cultural institutions. The ZPD offers a basis for understanding virtually all human growth in cognition and skill, particularly the development of language, through collaborations involving the experiences and knowledge of "more capable peers." In cultural institutions, where information is mediated by professionals, texts, interventions, juxtapositions, and patterns designed by more advanced others (librarians, curators, educators), Vygotsky's metaphor suggests a way to understand how learning happens through the words and structures of human relationships. The seminal ideas of Vygotsky, who died as a young man in 1934, illuminate our need to think about the intimate design of incremental, individual, interactive encounters for learning.

Note

1. There are several reference works that I encourage committed learners to consult, however, if they wish to understand the issues, discourse, and research record related to learning over the lifespan. Cultural institutions are marginal topics in nearly all of the following tools, but they hold large concepts and ideas of extraordinary relevance.

In the *International Encyclopedia of Adult Education and Training*, ed. Albert C. Tuijnman (Amsterdam: Elsevier, 1996), one can find extensive entries on such entries as "Lifelong Learning," "Lifespan Development," "Learning Transfer," and "Community Education and Community Development." To extend these themes, see also the *International Handbook of Lifelong Learning* (Dordrecht: Kluwer, 2001, 2 vols.). Although it is now dated, one of the most valuable tools is the *Encyclopedia of Educational Research*, ed. Marvin C. Alkin (New York: Macmillan, 1992, 4 vols.), produced under the authority of the American Educational Research Association. I find that the *International Encyclopedia of Communications*, ed. Erik Barnouw (New York: Oxford University Press, 1989, 4 vols.) and the *Encyclopedia of Communication and Information*, ed. Jorge Reina Schement (New York: Macmillan, 2002, 3 vols.) are relevant to much that cultural institutions do. The new edition of the *International Encyclopedia of the Behavioral and Social Sciences*, eds. Neil Smelser and Paul Balthes (Amsterdam: Elsevier, 2001, 25 vols.), is an intellectual monument and a magnificent reference tool, holding immense value for an informed social life.

Appendix B: To Observe

In order to develop fresh observations among my students in cultural institutions, I have offered these broad observational guidelines, derived from the rich and important work of such scholars as Egon Guba, Yvonna Lincoln, Norman Denzin, and Robert Stake.[1]

Notes for Entering and Describing a Cultural Institution

Approach the environment with a minimum of preparation, or with no preparation at all.

- Suspend judgments, avoid early closure. Even if you have been present before, strive to make this experience fresh.
- Clarify your anticipations and hopes. Remember the values that bring you to the threshold. If you are evaluating, be clear about your observational framework and the assumptions in your stance. Write these things down before you enter.

Monitor your impressions with care.

- Keep an account of impressions as they evolve. Pause and review after an hour; begin again on a new page. Let things happen as you observe, and interfere with nothing. The institution is a working organization; it will take time to see it work, and more time to see its patterns.
- Examine the setting fully, noting the human beings in the scene, their individual activities, the objects at hand, and any tools or other materials in play.[2]
- Determine the overall situation and its limits, the actions and interactions apparent in the situation, the space available for special activities, talk, movement, or solitary reflection.
- Look for places where information is provided in the form of pamphlets, books, guides, labels, or directions.

Document what you observe in enough detail for you to revisit the experience later.

- Write, draw, photograph, tape record . . .
- Make notes of small and large observations that seem to be important; use a small notebook or annotate a guide or brochure. What is going on here? What words do you hear others using? What words of your own seem most fitting to describe the scene and its actions?

Accept little about the assumptions, purposes

- Do not attempt to match the situation you see with

or values of the environment as they are given in goals and mission statements; use the situation to define these for yourself.

the advertisements and promises of the institution; assume nothing about its character that you have not directly found evidence to believe. What you experience should define the setting, its values and atmosphere, and its apparent priorities.

- Develop the possible meanings of what you observe, and the assumptions and purposes that apparently guide the institution, according to what your senses tell you.

When you are ready, tentatively state the purposes, issues, or values that appear to drive the environment.

- Based on initial impressions and observations, it is useful to attempt to articulate . . .

  1. *The scope of the environment.* What are its boundaries? What does it include and exclude? What is its single primary theme? Can you find secondary and tertiary themes?

  2. *The information of the environment.* What data are available to the senses? What ideas are offered in the situation, verbal and nonverbal? How does the institution offer written data? How do programs or services enhance or extend support for the user's experiences?

  3. *The behaviors of the environment.* What acts, attitudes, or procedures does the

environment encourage or reward? What does one actually have to do to learn something here?

4. *The thinking encouraged or invited by the environment.* How does the place stimulate new thoughts about its contents?

Examine smaller, more specific contexts after the larger contexts have been described. In these smaller contexts, strive to identify themes and ideas that define the collection.

- Observe in selected smaller spaces where users pause to make choices and pay closer attention to the order of things.
- In concentrated places, it is easier to attend to the detailed components of what is given to the user. Collections can be examined separately and seen as parts of the whole setting.
- Human behaviors can be observed closely in such frames. Consider face-to-face exchanges and uses of language to ask questions or solve problems. What choices are open to users? How easy is it to communicate here?
- Vary experiences over time; alternately focus on two specific locations and compare them.
- Look for consistent ideas from place to place. Are there patterns of design or structure in what you observe? Are any organizing principles or constant questions evident?
- How is this like or unlike other parts of the setting?

Identify the possible center of the entire setting—a place or a person, an instrument or a tool, an object or an artifact, a class or category of things— that can be used to explain other parts of the setting.[3]	• What themes or issues tend to unify the observed parts of the institution? How do all of the felt impressions, documented ideas, and observed behaviors come together? • How do these later themes compare to early observations of the setting? How have later observations altered earlier perspectives?
Summarize and begin to communicate what you have observed.	• Emphasize the situation as a place of learning. • Provide details, descriptions of experiences, notes from the field. Begin with your original thoughts about the environment, before you entered it. • Do not reduce observations to abstractions. Place yourself at the center of the situation, thinking of the user's experiences as you have seen them.

Questions are guiding instruments. Every person who examines a cultural institution might usefully address several questions from a naive user's perspective, asking them in such a way that what is *thought to be obvious* must be articulated—given words. Ten guiding questions follow.

1. What kinds of thinking or reflective learning might happen here?

2. What sustained behaviors or new activities would each of these kinds of thinking or reflective learning require the user to carry out?

3. What forms of information are given in the situation, specifically to nourish these behaviors or thoughts?

4. In this setting, how might a person use the information given?

5. What are the most prominent forms of structure or order present, such as chronology, geography, or a classification scheme?

6. How does the setting invite the independent learner?

7. What do these invitations and forms of assistance assume about the institution's users?

8. What themes or unifying ideas are evident in this setting? Do they connect to institutions other than this one?

9. What connections does the setting create between itself and everyday life, outside the institution?

10. In what ways, and under what conditions, is this a lifelong resource?

Naive questions illuminate. A first field observation should be a very general experience; it allows the observer to think about the apparent purposes of a site. Why does it exist? What do you understand its mission to be? What do its sponsors, designers, and administrators want to have happen here? An observer begins with the simplest, most visible elements of the setting, but will always move toward less visible activities as well. What is going on here—in the literal sense of the flow of activity? What do people do? Where do they pause? Do they speak? What do they say?

The observer changes nothing. Other than entering the setting, the observer does not interrupt the flow of activity. The observer does not interrogate others, does not draw attention, and does not make notes in the presence of the observed. If possible, the observer leaves no traces. The observer respects and does not compromise the pri-

vacy and independence of the setting, or a person's opportunity to experience it.

Observations deepen quickly. Consider the less visible activities
in the setting as well. What kinds of thinking might the environment inspire? How does information appear to its
users? How easily does this information relate to the
world outside the room? In this place, how might you define the overall process that is occurring? What is *the continuity of the environment*, the flow of activity and thought
that is most apparent?

Reflect on observations privately. Spend time apart, reviewing
notes and adding to the documentation. It is likely that
further questions will lead you back to the setting for additional observations. The more one looks at a complex situation, the more one sees and feels about it.

The human being is the instrument of inquiry. Data enter the observer's consciousness, and the observer interprets and
records what is apparent in the scene. The observer is
present and engaged, but more attentive to the other human beings, and to the structures in the environment than
to its content. In intense fieldwork, an observer is present
for a long time—hours, perhaps, or days, or weeks—
attempting to understand the smallest activity and its
meaning. But in order to understand a cultural institution's general purposes and values, a far less intense immersion can be quite effective.

We interpret constantly. We are not in a laboratory, awaiting
the arrival of data from the outside world, or disassem-
bling an artifact or specimen to see its heart. We are observing a scene as it changes. As we observe, we think; as
we think, we interpret; as we interpret, we lead ourselves
toward concepts and ideas of what we have seen. For
many inquirers, these are the most useful processes of inquiry when we hope to understand how and why people
do what they do. In some cases, we may think of this as
problem-finding inquiry. When we identify a possible research issue through our observations, we are ready to ask
new questions from a different perspective and method.

Notes

1. See, for example, Egon Guba, *Toward a Methodology of Naturalistic Inquiry in Educational Evaluation* (Los Angeles: Center for the Study of Evaluation, UCLA Graduate School of Education, 1978); and Robert E. Stake, *The Art of Case Study Research* (Thousand Oaks, Calif.: Sage, 1995). Norman Denzin and Yvonna Lincoln's *Handbook of Qualitative Research* (Thousand Oaks, Calif.: Sage, 1994) is the best reference tool for further investigation of qualitative inquiry perspective and method.

2. The value of observations in natural settings is always secondary to the rights of the observed to privacy and integrity. An observer always observes unobtrusively, discreetly, and respectfully, and does not place the individuals observed at risk by identifying them in writing or through photography. Guidelines for establishing this integrity—for observations, surveys, interviews, and other forms of data gathering— are available from many social science organizations and university boards for the protection of human subjects.

3. At the American Museum of Natural History, I wandered around the exhibits for several weeks before I understood this principle. I found a center of the museum in its highly didactic exhibits devoted (very briefly) to the origins of the universe and the beginnings of invertebrate life. I could also take concepts evident in this space (adaptation, evolution, specialization) and apply them to exhibitions throughout the rest of the museum, including exhibitions of human growth, culture, and civilization. (Revisiting photographs of the exhibit, twenty years later, it is impossible to understand how the density of information could be processed by anyone standing up and reading for hours, as I did. Later, in the museum shop, I purchased a small volume in the Golden Guide series devoted to evolution and annotated it with indications of where museum exhibits could be used to demonstrate the concepts it described.)

Appendix C: Each Life: Cultural Institutions and Civic Engagement

As this morning spreads across the nation, we can imagine the opening of about 40,000 doors and gates to public and academic libraries, museums, history centers and sites, gardens, arboreta, zoos and aquaria, many more small archival collections, and countless exhibitions in neighborhoods and centers of American community pride.

As we imagine these doors opening, we also imagine the people of those American places entering and beginning to search for something they require.

The American Library Association, reports that 1,146,284,000 visits were made to public libraries in 2000, and in a survey of 1,000 citizens, nearly all expressed the belief that "libraries and librarians play an essential role in our democracy and are needed now more than ever."

The American Association of Museums notes that "American museums average approximately 865 million visits per year or 2.3 million visits"—probably 5 million museum hours—every day.

Each year in our nation, there are two billion library users and museum users combined. This morning—in North Carolina, Indiana, Texas, California, Hawaii, Alaska—something is beginning, something is going on in the cultural institutions of our nation.

What do such places, in such communities, contain?

- Traces of individual lives lived right in that place

- Records of institutions and the faces of those who built them—ghostly faces in sepia photographs

- Documents of the free associations that shaped that place: trade unions, congregations, fire departments, immigrant societies, tribes, quilting circles

- Objects and knowledge assembled and preserved in the name of the people, who use the collection for every reason

Human beings are there as well—collection designers and builders, who, thinking of the past living into the present and the present living into the future, opened the doors and gates this morning.

This is where we find

- Evidence of knowledge in the midst of mysteries

- Images of how work is done by human hands—how one handmade life is a breathing document of genius

- The cumulated insights of eyewitnesses, praise singers, record keepers

And we find human beings who give what humans give: voices, questions, and the keys to every learning life: integrity, generosity, and kindness.

In John W. Gardner's word, they offer us *self-renewal*, so we can do the hardest thing: *to think again*. They remind us of the ideas and responsibilities that linger whenever we associate with each other in service and mutual aid. They confirm our place in a narrative: our own, our family, our community, our national story. They provide evidence that we can become authors of our own knowledge. They make possible a fearless view of complexity.

They contain systems, living and not; objects and books to be read; paper and electronic tools; works of craft, works of art—all in conversation with us. Wendell Berry writes: "Works of art participate in our lives; we are not just distant observers of *their* lives. They are in conversation among themselves and with us. This is a part of the description of human life; we do the way we do partly because of things said to us by works of art, and because of things that we have said in reply."[1]

What are these conversations about? Every common theme in the course of life: family, home, the heart; compassion, hope, learning, change; crisis, frailty, conflict; despair.

But each life at the door this morning is undespairing and unfinished. Each carries its questions, begun in the family, or in school, religion, reading, or conversation. Each life gives them energy and makes them new questions this morning.

We live in the midst of generations; we know that learning never ends. It grows, deepens, and widens all at once. People find courage, trust, and insight in themselves as they find knowledge. This is our communal work: only by building ourselves among others can we become ourselves; only by believing in the value of others can we find value in ourselves.

Every opportunity to gather information and establish a fair point of view nourishes consideration and conscience. Weaving our many-stranded experiences into a community story enhances empathy and responsibility to others. As information and complexity increase, the likelihood of understanding entire patterns of life increases as well.

At our best, we live up to what we have been given to solve in our lives; then we go beyond it—we make something greater of it; we make something more of ourselves through it. Alan Wolfe writes about "the capacity of Americans to reinvent their world . . . to tinker with families, neighborhoods, and churches, searching for new forms that provide for both tradition and modernity, freedom and community."[2]

Public cultural institutions are the treasures of the community, and the engaged citizen is the treasure of the institution. The civic enterprise does not require giants; it requires learners. It doesn't require heroes; it requires the everyday habits of curiosity, a little edginess and impatience. It requires people who are more than smart: they know their empty places and how to fill them. But the civic culture will need people who are smart no more than it will require people who are generous, forgiving, and kind.

Civic culture *requires* people who understand the deep motions of human experiences, because our civic engagements are grounded in an understanding of other lives than our own; we are united in equal possession and authorship of American culture. Our cultural institutions give us this: a concept of the whole enterprise of our world, vast and only partially charted, yet grounded in what we know intimately: our towns and cities, and ourselves.

Democracy *requires* us to be open, unfinished, human works. Emily Dickinson, model of that rare courage able to flourish in a still, small room, writes "I dwell in Possibility."[3] Quietly extending this legacy, Eudora Welty writes these final words in her memoir: "All serious daring starts from within."[4]

When the gates are open in cultural institutions it is never to late to dare, or to dwell in possibility. We observe and explore; we become apprentices to each other; storytellers, mapmakers, and craftspeople as well. We craft our own truths. We seek the outcome of our own stories; we look for convivial paths and tools; we marvel when we are given a rare glimpse of mastery. In this way we come to understand where in our-*selves* mastery resides.

Jean Bethke Elshtain writes, "Civil society creates spaces for the enactment of human projects."[5] She refers to "commitments and ties that locate the citizen in bonds of trust, reciprocity, mutuality, competence for the task at hand."[6]

Civic energies can be sustained only if we have learning and renewal in our neighborhoods, and anticipation at their edges, where we encounter each other in the civil play of civic engagement. In our museums and libraries we construct forums for the play of a culture—the emotions, the dramas, the dialogues, the trying out of our untried lives.

In Tracy Kidder's *Home Town*,[7] we see that a living community is always in transition, moving not toward some great particular future, but in delicate adaptation to the immediate

moment. Cultural institutions, though they are always secondary to human patience and courage, exist to help us to move
ourselves—and therefore our communities—to the edges of the
possible.

In such ways, democracy, based on the free exchange of information, is proven in the world. In our local institutions we
touch and illuminate each other as we exchange information, because the table of our community is so small. When we sit
around that table and present ourselves to each other, when we
take our memberships and serve, we are more than ourselves
alone. Some part of democratic structures must always say to
each life: This is a form of constructive trust of which we all are
capable.

We understand our community best by understanding what
it wants to have happen, for itself and for all of its citizens; by
what it keeps, from generation to generation; and by how freely
knowledge is shared as a community possession.

Why do we do this? Wendell Berry answers, "We are up
against mystery."[8] He writes, "We are wholly dependent on a
pattern . . . that we partly understand."[9]

Berry also writes about an artifact, an old bucket, hanging for
fifty years on a fence post.

> However small a landmark the old bucket is, it is not trivial. It
> is one of the signs by which I know my country and myself.
> And to me it is irresistibly suggestive in the way it collects
> leaves and other woodland sheddings as they fall through
> time. It collects stories, too, as they fall through time. . . . It is
> doing in a passive way what a human community must do ac-
> tively and thoughtfully. A human community, too, must collect
> leaves and stories, and turn them to account. It must build soil,
> and build [the] memory of itself . . . that will be its culture.[10]
>
> When a community loses its memory, its members no
> longer know one another. How can they know one another if
> they have forgotten or have never learned one another's sto-
> ries? If they do not know one another's stories, how can they
> know whether or not to trust one another? People who do not
> trust one another do not help one another, and moreover they
> fear one another.[11]

We turn to the authentic, for strength and energy; to lived lives and living experiences, for evidences of human integrity; and, to the mirror of our own questions, we turn to see that *who we are* allows us to imagine *who we might yet become*. Ultimately, we turn to these things in order to turn toward each other.

This is the America of Whitman and Emerson, grounded in the people of a place, finding regeneration and replenishment in conversations and artifacts of the physical world, restoring to ourselves a wild, inspired imagination of something previously hidden.

It is for that uncertain hidden thing that we must now look as a culture. As we know, in our throes of loss and resilience, public culture is a form of healing, the promise of solace, a finding out of where one is, and—at times to see through tears—of what great thing one is a certain part.

American cultural institutions are the only extensive civic structures in the world whose authority and integrity exist to evoke trust, possibility, and reflection in the life of each citizen; they are critical agents in our imagination of a democracy, where democracy will always begin.

We need to stop thinking of museums and libraries as places where we keep *things* safe; we need to see them as places where we are *ourselves* made safe, and strengthened, and where we may safely become what we have not yet been.

Notes

This work was presented at The White House Colloquium on Libraries, Museums, and Lifelong Learning, October 29, 2002. The data in the early sentences of this essay were gathered in October 2002 from the websites of the American Library Association, the American Association of Museums, the American Association for State and Local History, the American Association of Botanical Gardens and Arboreta, the American Zoo and Aquarium Association, and the National Park Service.

1. Wendell Berry, "Style and Grace," in *What Are People For?* (New York: North Point Press, 1990), 64.

2. Alan Wolfe, "Is Civil Society Obsolete?," in *Community Works: The Revival of Civil Society in America,*. ed. E. J. Dionne, Jr. (Washington, D.C.: Brookings Institution Press, 1998), 22.

3. Emily Dickinson, *The Complete Poems of Emily Dickinson* (New York: Little, Brown, 1960), 327.

4. Eudora Welty, "One Writer's Beginnings," in *Stories, Essays & Memoir* (New York: The Library of America, 1998), 948 [Harvard University Press, 1984].

5. Jean Bethke Elshtain, "Not a Cure-All," in *Community Works: The Revival of Civil Society in America*, ed. E. J. Dionne, Jr. (Washington, D.C.: Brookings Institution Press, 1998), 28.

6. Elshtain, "Not a Cure-All," 25.

7. Tracy Kidder, *Home Town* (New York: Random House, 1999).

8. Wendell Berry, *Home Economics* (New York: North Point Press, 1987), ix, 4.

9. Berry, *Home Economics*, ix.

10. Wendell Berry, "The Work of Local Culture," in *What Are People For?* (New York: North Point Press, 1990), 154.

11. Berry, "The Work of Local Culture," 157.

Index

apprenticeship, 82–86
Arendt, Hannah, 62
autonomy in museums, 26–27;
    for children, 142–49

Barber, Bernard, 121–22
Bellah, Robert N., 58
Berry, Wendell, 64
Bradley, Bill, 53n2
Bruner, Jerome S., 57, 72, 88, 150,
    152n7, 178

children: as learners in museums,
    83, 131–53; experiences in
    museums, 143–47
cognition, situated, 79–82
collections, 45–48, 66
communication, 72–73
community, 39–40, 55–68
concept inventory, 78–79
concept map. See map, concept
configuration of education
    (Cremin), 179
construction for learning,
    museum as, 1–3

contexts, 30
Cremin, Lawrence A., xiii, 179
critical thinking, 137–38
Csikszentmihalyi, Mihalyi, 86,
    150, 180
cultural institution: and
    community, 59–63; defined,
    xiv–xv; themes, 56–57

Dalai Lama, 128
Dana, John Cotton, xviii, 66
Dervin, Brenda, 73
Dewey, John, 41, 181, 190
Duckworth, Eleanor, 83–84

Eco, Umberto, 11
education and schooling, 58–60,
    168–69
educative museum defined, 18
Eisner, Elliot, 2
Emerson, Ralph Waldo, 206
Ennis, Robert, 72
Erikson, Erik H., 181
ethics, 109–30
experiences, emancipatory, 5

fabric metaphor, 7–8
Farnham-Diggory, Sylvia, 84–85
Flow (Csikszentmihalyi), 180
forum, 28, 35, 37–38, 49, 52,
    61–62, 87, 167

Gaither, Edmund Barry, 59
Gardner, Howard, 85–86, 182–83
Gardner, John W., 138, 183
Geertz, Clifford, 14, 62, 64
Govier, Trudy, 110, 124–25
Greenblatt, Stephen, 9–10
Greene, Maxine, 3, 62, 183–84
Guillevic, Eugene, 162

heuristic, 171

Illich, Ivan, 184–85
incendiary institutions, 37, 49
information given, 74
information in museums, 9,
    25–26, 44–45, 50
inquiry, xv, 60–61

John-Steiner, Vera, 185

Karp, Ivan, 59
knowledge: construction,
    152–53n8; in museums, 20–22;
    public, xix; structure, xv, 25,
    72
Knox, Alan, 97
Kosuth, Joseph, 14
Krippendorff, Klaus, 72

language, 6, 25, 43
Lave, Jean and Etienne Wenger,
    185–86
learning, 51–52, 69–70, 72; adult,
    xv, xvi; beyond museums, 26,

27, 31–32, 42, 74, 127, 139;
    enemies of, 165–70; lifelong,
    43; support for, 24–28. See also
    experiences, emancipatory
libraries and museums, xviii,
    41–49, 71–73
Lipman, Matthew, 152n6
literacy, 60

map, concept, 76–79
memory, 42–43, 76
Merwin, W. S., 39
Mezirow, Jack, 5, 186
Miller, Sam, 66
museum problem solving, 22–23,
    29–32
museum user: defined, 19–20;
    skills, 29–31

Neruda, Pablo, 95–96
Noddings, Nel, 187

objects, 30
open work, museum as, 2–3, 4,
    11–13

pursuit skills, 148–49

questions, 6, 9, 30, 33–34, 38–39,
    83, 93–108, 132–34, 157–58

Resnick, Lauren, 60
Richards, I. A., 96
Rilke, Rainer Maria, 155, 161
Rogoff, Barbara, 87–88, 105,
    187–88

scholarship, xv
Schön, Donald, 8, 188–89
Smith, Frank, 6, 8, 137, 167, 189

society, civil, 39–40, 53n2; and
cultural institutions, 59–60, 65,
159
Sterling, Peter, 12–13
story, 14, 65, 79
survival skills, 149

Tharp, Roland G. and Ronald
Gallimore, 146–47
thinking in museums, 31; critical
thinking, 137–38
tools, 51–52, 61
Tough, Allen, 189
trust, 109–30, 159

unfinished issues, 17, 94, 162
user needs, 20, 23–24

Vygotsky, Lev, 6, 12, 82–83, 110,
150, 190

Wenger. *See* Lave, Jean and
Etienne Wenger
Whitman, Walt, 206

zone of competence (Brown and
Reeve), 83
zone of proximal development
(Vygotsky), 82, 146, 190

About the Author

David Carr speaks and writes as an advocate for critical thinking and reflective practice in libraries, museums, and other cultural institutions. As an inquirer, educator, and consultant, he has observed, spoken, and listened in many of the strongest and most thoughtful American cultural settings. His essays, articles, and reviews have appeared in *Museum News, Curator, Public Libraries,* and in other journals and collections.

Holding an undergraduate degree from Drew University; master's degrees from Teachers College, Columbia University, and Rutgers, the State University of New Jersey; and a Ph.D. from Rutgers, the author has taught librarians and other educators for thirty-five years. He currently serves on the faculty of the School of Information and Library Science at the University of North Carolina, Chapel Hill, where he teaches about reference tools, collection building, and the topics of these essays: information, culture, and the professional imagination.

Among his research interests are the habits and practices of reading; how we understand and use contexts; relationships between tools and cognition; critical thinking in the presence of information; and the use of naive questions and heuristic concepts in museum settings. In 1994, he received a national award for teaching excellence from the Association for Library and Information Science Education, and in 2001 he received a similar honor from his students at Chapel Hill.